# TIGRANES THE GREAT

# About the Author

Serge Momjian was born in Beirut in 1946. He moved to London in the 1970s and studied journalism then took a degree course in creative writing.

He has worked as a reporter, covering arts and culture for major publications, including Beirut's *Daily Star* (the Middle East's leading English-language newspaper) and London's *Events* magazine. His feature articles have been translated and published in the Armenian press. By the time he reached his forties, he was devoting his time to writing novels. His works, all published in the United Kingdom, include *Conflicting Motives*, *The Invisible Line*, *The Singer of the Opera*, *Memories of the Past*, *Komitas: The Artist and The Martyr*, and *Gateway to Armenia*.

In recognition of his biographical *Komitas* book, which included dialogue for the first time and was written in commemoration of the centenary of the Armenian Genocide, he was awarded the William Saroyan medal in 2015 by the Ministry of Diaspora of the Republic of Armenia (RA). During his literary career his innovative writings have brought him praise and a good reputation.

# TIGRANES THE GREAT
## The Rise and Fall of an Ancient Empire

A comprehensive historical biography

**By Serge Momjian**

**HEDDON PUBLISHING**
United Kingdom

First published in Great Britain 2020 by Heddon Publishing

www.heddonpublishing.com

Copyright © Serge Momjian 2020

A catalogue record for this book is available from the British Library

ISBN 978-1-913166-24-3

All rights reserved. No part of this publication may be reproduced, stored in a retrieval system or transmitted in any form or by any means, electric, mechanical, photocopying, recording or otherwise, without the prior permission of the publisher.

This is a biographical work based on true history with real historical characters. Includes appendices for data, maps and images.

The right of Serge Momjian to be identified as the author of this work has been asserted by him in accordance with the Copyright, Designs and Patents Act 1988.

Cover Design: Serge Momjian and Catherine Clarke

Cover images from People Of Ar, Wikimedia Commons-Gaba, Desktop-Blue A. Andrees, Ferrell Jenkings

Coin images from Coin Archives

This work is first dedicated to the Almighty God, the source of inspiration to write a book on Tigranes the Great, to friends who have encouraged me to include dialogue again in the new work, and to the people of Armenia and its Diaspora communities.

# Contents

Chapter 1: Prince Tigranes as a hostage in Parthia

Chapter 2: His coronation in Artaxata

Chapter 3: King Tigranes' first campaign

Chapter 4: Mithridates VI, King of Pontus

Chapter 5: The Alliance between Pontus and Armenia

Chapter 6: The royal hunt

Chapter 7: Tigranes' military involvement in Cappadocia

Chapter 8: His conquests of Mesopotamian Kingdoms

Chapter 9: The First Mithridatic War

Chapter 10: The expansion of Tigranes' kingdom

Chapter 11: The Second Mithridatic War, his poison elixir

Chapter 12: The fortress city of Tigranocerta

Chapter 13: The Third Mithridatic War

Chapter 14: The first revolt by one of Tigranes' sons

Chapter 15: Tigranes' conquest of Phoenicia

Chapter 16: His audience with Appius Claudius

Chapter 17: Preparation for war

Chapter 18: The battle of Tigranocerta

Chapter 19: Encounter between Mithridates and Tigranes

Chapter 20: Their involvement in guerrilla warfare

Chapter 21: Mithridates' final collapse

Chapter 22: The meeting between Pompey and Tigranes

Chapter 23: Death of Mithridates

Chapter 24: A review of past experiences by Tigranes

Epilogue:     Page 139

Appendices:  Page 145 to 173

# Acknowledgements

I would like to thank Katharine Smith (the Editor) and Catherine Clark (the Cover Designer) for their patience and skills throughout the production process, and Nathalie Kulkhanjian for additional assistance in the cover designing.

My thanks also go to Joshua J. Mark (Author/Researcher) at *Ancient History Encyclopedia*, to Michael Roaf (Ancient Iranian Studies), and to Adrian Goldsworthy (Ancient Roman History) for their various comments on the Ancient Near East from the end of the second century BC to the first century BC.

# Cover Images

In the centre, Tigranes' tiara (headdress) split in the middle.
Bottom-left: the bust of Mithridates VI, King of Pontus.
Bottom-middle: Zoroastrian fire altar.
Bottom-right: The Roman legions.

# A Note to the Reader

Speaking about the genre of the book, this is not historical fiction but a political biography based on true history with real historical figures. As explained in the Preface, direct dialogue, partly corroborated, and partly representative but placed in the historical context, is included in the book. The idea is to bring the ancient past to life.

It is hoped that this work will be accessible to those who love history but may never have read about Tigranes' reign.

# Preface

Tigranes the Great, a powerful member of the Royal House of Artaxiad, and of Persian-Alan ancestry, ruled the Kingdom of Armenia from 95 to 55 BC. His coronation took place in his homeland, after his release from the Parthian court, where he had been held as a privileged hostage. He was a very ambitious and audacious ruler, known for his magnificent silver coinage – the first ever struck by a monarch of Armenian descent. On coming to the throne, he consolidated his power, and appointed feudal lords to important posts within his monarchical domains, in a decentralized system.

At the request of Mithridates VI, Eupator and King of Pontus, Tigranes forged a political alliance with him, to secure each other's flanks from the expansion of Rome. The signed treaty was enforced by the marriage of Tigranes to Cleopatra, the daughter of Mithridates. However, Tigranes had no intention of being directly involved in his ally's military campaigns with the Roman state. He had his own agenda, for expanding his kingdom fully independent of the constraints imposed upon him by the regional powers.

Tigranes' forces invaded the neighbouring dynastic kingdoms under Parthian rule – one invasion was followed by another – in what became a growing imperial war of conquests. Within a decade or so, a huge area was ravaged as the king occupied all their lands, making their realms and peoples his vassals. Those victories eventually enabled him to take the proud Achaemenid title of "King of Kings".

Around 69 BC, Armenia was emerging as a new Eastern power, amid the ruins of the decaying Seleucid kingdom. Tigranes reached the peak of his historical fame and glory. His kingdom was transformed, for a brief and spectacular period, into a mighty empire that stretched from the Caspian and Black Seas to the Eastern Mediterranean Sea, and from Media (north-western Iran) to Cilicia (the south-eastern coast of modern Turkey).

Cicero, a Roman statesman and orator, said: "Tigranes made the Republic of Rome tremble before the prowess of his arms." The Roman historian, Marcus Velleius Paterculus called Tigranes the Great "the most powerful king of his era" and "the greatest of all the kings".

Tigranes' reign had marked the apex of Hellenization, with an equally strong Iranian undercurrent, which he shared with Pontus and the neighbouring states of the Near East. Those states kept their various languages and, together with Tigranes' domains, preserved the primitive aristocratic pattern of multiple para-feudal principalities. The capital, Tigranocerta, named after the king, lay in the centre of the empire, to the south of the Armenian plateau. It had been a Hellenistic city, with a royal palace, a theatre, and pagan temples situated near the citadel. The official language at the time was Greek, alongside Persian and Aramaic, for Greek rhetoricians and philosophers were welcomed to the royal court, and Greek actors were invited to the amphitheatre to perform comedies and dramas.

Tigranes (Tigrana), a name of Persian origin, meaning "fighting with arrows", was in fact an absolute Hellenistic monarch, with a strong Persian outlook. An Armenian only by the royal bloodline of Artaxiad, he had very few, if any, of the so-called Armenian character traits and patriotic sentiments overenthusiastically expressed in modern Armenian literary works. Like many other contemporary kings in Ancient Asia, he was a slave-owner, and practised polygamy. His empire was his personal property, rather than the peoples', who were only exploited and engaged in his imperial war of conquests, and bore no love for their emperor, whose ultimate aim was to unite many territories and peoples under one ruler.

Unfortunately, as a result of domestic dissensions, Tigranes' goal for keeping peace within his domains was cut short. He regularly had to overcome opposition from the feudal nobility of the aristocrats, although he was not fully confident of their loyalty to him. He also had to face multiple revolts of his power-hungry sons, who attempted unsuccessfully to seize the throne. Moreover, he had to ensure that the population of the devastated regions, whom he forcibly transferred to his new capital city, would not fall prey to conspiracies from other feudal states.

Meanwhile, the Romans cared little about the Hellenistic high ideals in the Ancient Near East. Most importantly, they could not allow any nation to challenge their power and interests. But there is more to it than that. Neither Lucullus nor Pompey hesitated to pursue their political ambition to dominate the region for Roman supremacy, where enormous wealth awaited them.

Outside of the world of prominent historians, scholars and academicians, as well as Armenia and its diaspora communities, Tigranes the Great remains almost unknown. He is, however, a well-established historical figure in modern scholarly research. This book, a credible and fair account of Tigranes' reign, is intended precisely for general audiences. It explores his royal life and fate and delineates the Pontic king's military conflicts with Rome in parts, because of their alliance, family ties, and neighbouring states.

I have been inspired to write about Tigranes firstly by the wish to provide a realistic portrayal of this Oriental ruler, revealing his true colours. Secondly, by his dynamic personality and adventurous spirit, which sit alongside triumph, power and influence. Like Alexander the Great, Tigranes was a man of culture and a promoter of Hellenistic civilization, who left an everlasting mark on history. Although this great military leader of immense vigour and stubborn will eventually lost his empire in a humiliating capitulation, he continued to be the national epic hero and symbol of Armenia.

In general, dialogue is a very useful tool that makes fictitious characters more lifelike, and the situation more immediate. Adding direct dialogue to non-fiction or historical biography to bring real characters to life is a challenging but rewarding experience, for it can greatly enhance the work. In my case, since I want to include some dialogue for the first time, it is imperative to consider a number of things. First, I need to make sure that my dialogue is in the context of known facts – the locations, the people and the events – and meets that criteria in order to be within the bounds of historical accuracy. Second, I have to verify that I am protected by reliable documents which corroborate my dialogue, some of which, however, is representative, and does not have to be verbatim. In other words, it gets at a larger truth, even though it must sacrifice those smaller truths. In some parts of the story, I extrapolate tidbits from ancient literary sources and use my own logic to work out what might have happened in this or that scene.

This book is a re-interpretation and reconstruction of the historic account of Tigranes' imperial reign. It is important to me to give readers, along with the storyline, a condensed description of the Ancient Near East (the first civilizations) to understand how it revealed itself, religiously, socially, culturally and politically, from the end of the second century BC to Tigranes' rule in the first century BC. There is, of course, no definitive historical biography or a definitive account of a historical figure, for there will always be things that remain a mystery. Most importantly, I approached my subject and characters in all good faith. (see Appendices for data or details, maps, images, and sketch).

S.M

# Main Characters

Tigranes II the Great: King of Armenia
Mithridates VI: Eupator and King of Pontus
Cleopatra of Pontus: Queen consort of Armenia
Lucius Lucullus: Roman General
Pompey the Great: Roman General

# PART ONE
# The Rise

# CHAPTER 1

In 120 BC, Mithridates II, King of Parthia, defeated King Artavasdes I of Armenia, and eventually deposed him, after being repelled in several previous attempts to invade his kingdom. By order of the Parthian king, guards captured the young Prince Tigranes, the son of Artavasdes' brother, Tigranes I, who then ascended to the throne of the Artaxiad dynasty. While the shocked prince was pulled by his captors towards three horses, he asked in surprise where he was being taken, but received no reply.

The two mounted guards; one in front of the mounted prince, the other at the rear, rode all three southward at full gallop. The following day, they left the Armenian lands and moved further to the south. The prince was in disbelief at what was happening to him. After travelling about 300 miles in five days, they reached the city of Ctesiphon, which was the principal royal residence of the Parthian kings.

The Prince of Armenia had remained in the king's court as a hostage guest. On the first day, he felt angry, trapped and helpless. But, as the members of the court treated him with respect and courtesy, these emotions gradually disappeared. He was educated in Parthian culture, which comprised elements of Greek culture. In fact, the Arsacid rulers affirmed they were also Philhellenes – friends of Greeks – and the Greek alphabet legends were inscribed on their coins. The court minstrel gave performances including recitations of poetry and oral literature, accompanied by music.

In the following months, Tigranes received military training under an instructor, which included horsemanship, horse grooming, archery, and at a later stage hunting. From his military masters, who were renowned for their warrior ethos, Tigranes learned how to wage campaigns.

The government of the Parthian Empire was a decentralized political system based on Achaemenid precedents – a mere conglomerate of subkingdoms, provinces, and vassal states – with tense relationships among rival ethnic groups. The empire, being culturally and politically heterogeneous, contained a variety of votive religious beliefs, the most widespread being those dedicated to the Greek and Persian cults, which were often blended together as one, and received daily and monthly offerings. A considerable number of the women at the court were royal concubines taken as captives, slaves, gifts, or as part of political alliances.

Ruled by a feudalistic military elite, garrisons were permanently maintained at border forts. A trusted guard from the elite of the infantry was in charge of the protection of the king. Known as "the Great" in antiquity, he was a vigorous ruler, who assumed the traditional Persian Achaemenid title of "King of Kings". Mithridates II was one of the true creators of the Parthian state, after

Mithridates I and Phraates II, winning for it military and economic victories and raising it to a level comparable to that of the Achaemenian Empire.

At the zenith of his power, the new Parthian king's empire achieved a position of stability previously unknown in the East or the West. He maintained diplomatic relations with the two greatest ancient world powers, Rome and China. Ambassadors from the Far East had come to the king to undertake projects for opening up trade routes across central Asia, one of which later became very famous as the Silk Road. During the following years, Tigranes observed that the Parthians derived much of their power and wealth from their amazing ability to control and police the major trade routes, while maintaining the best possible relations with their neighbours to the east and to the west. By this time, he had learned the fine art of diplomacy.

Parthia had no central standing army; a satrap would quickly mobilise his cavalry and neutralise any danger, in the event of a threat. The main striking forces were the cataphracts, who were recruited from the aristocratic class and equipped with lances and swords. The light cavalry was formed from among the commoner class. Dressed in tunics and baggy trousers, they acted as mounted archers. The Parthian tactic was that of harassing the enemy using a hit-and-run method. The cavalry would first engage the enemy in a fight, then pretend to retreat in disarray. Their adversaries would quickly break in their flanks and, while the Parthians retreated, their skilful archers at the back would shoot at the pursuing enemy.

There was another military tactic, known as the "Parthian shot". While in a feigned retreat, their archers would suddenly twist backwards on their horses in full gallop and shoot at the enemy chasing after them. During such spectacular military manoeuvres, the enemy would lose thousands of men, before stopping the disastrous chase. Tigranes saw what the Parthians had accomplished with their cavalry and thought it would be a good idea to use their battle tactics one day.

The Parthian period also included the royal hunt, shown in paintings, which was one of the main occupations of the nobility and the king. A large numbers of hounds were kept to assist in hunting. On occasion, Tigranes and some of the sons of the elite nobles accompanied the king on hunts, as an essential part of their education. During the expedition, the prince watched with interest how well his master, with a bow, arrows and a sword, chased and attacked such prey as leopards, bears and deer in the outskirts of the city. Hunting for mountain sheep and goats was primarily to provide a source of food and skin clothing. The Parthians adopted the Babylonian calendar and dated the years using the Arsacid Era in 247 BC. They also measured shorter periods of time either by the position of the sun or water clocks.

# CHAPTER 2

When King Tigranes I died in 95 BC, his son Prince Tigranes was the only heir to the throne of Artaxiad, although somewhat a latecomer, being in his mid-forties. Having spent his young adulthood – about twenty years – at Mithridates II's imperial court as a privileged hostage, the prince was forced to hand over to him the "seventy fertile valleys" in exchange for his freedom. As a result, the Parthian king exacted the cession of these valleys bordering Media (north-western Iran).

Tigranes cut short a planned stay in Babylon, and came to Artaxata, where he was expected to be enthroned as a compliant client ruler in the temporary presence of a Parthian delegation, to ensure the safe transference of power to their nominal ally. Artaxata was the Hellenized name of the ancient capital of Armenia, with some intervals, from 189 BC, and known as the "seat of the Artaxiads". Artaxias I (Artashes), grandfather of the new King Tigranes, once the satrap of the Seleucid empire, founded the Artaxiad dynasty – a branch of the Orontid (Eruandid) dynasty of Iranian origin from the sixth century BC.

During Tigranes' coronation rite as Tigranes II (a hereditary and dynastic title), he clothed himself in traditional Persian/Greek style – a toga over a long-sleeved white tunic, falling to the knees under his pearl belt. The king was then given his pearl-edged tiara (head-dress) in the triangular prism with five-pointed rays at its top – design belonging exclusively to the ancient Iranian world. An eight-pointed central star of divinity was flanked on either side by two eagles facing outward but with their heads turned towards each other – the Artaxiad coat of arms. Right underneath, a wide headband (diadem) encircled the monarchic tiara, with strips falling freely at the back of Tigranes' neck, his ears concealed beneath a pair of long earflaps, which were outlined with pearls.

The coronation ceremony associated with kingship took place in a temple, in the presence of dignitaries from the Artaxiad and Parthian Houses. It included an oath sworn by Tigranes, and the anointing of the new king by a high priest (Magus), representing a bestowal of consent upon his enthronement. After the return of the procession to the old royal palace of Artaxata, all the dignitaries paid homage to the king. That was followed in the evening by a joyful feast in celebration of both Tigranes' return from his captivity, and his coronation.

In the following days, the highly energetic and ambitious king rapidly began to rebuild and reorganize every aspect of socio-political, economic and military life. The society in the king's domains was feudal, combined with dynastic elements in a decentralized system. Since it was exceedingly difficult to exert control over a large territory – a combination of lofty mountains and deep river valleys – divided into provinces and independent powerful clans, the aim of the monarch was to preserve the society, rather than to govern it. Typical of Parthians, the noble families from various regions of Tigranes' domain were governed by their own and raised troops under their own command. In the course of time, these local rulers formed the aristocratic class in the country's society. Tribal chiefs, who were later incorporated into the nobility, which played a vital role, controlled vast tracts of land and acted as the king's intermediaries within their communities.

The growth of the social division of labour was the basis of the society's transition to the slaveholding economy. The upper classes – the nobility and wealthy elite – were dominated by the religion of Zoroastrianism, the fire worship of the chief gods with Parthian traits, Ahura Mazda and Mithras (known as Aramazd and Mher in Armenian mythology). The much lower classes remained loyal to the traditional worship of polytheism. Pagan shrine cults were built, housing numerous statues or images of deities that polytheist people had chosen to honour.

In fact, the rise of Parthia and its feudal aristocracy had exercised a major influence on the development of society and votive religion in Tigranes' and his predecessors' kingdom. As a result, a fruitful cultural interchange developed. Most of the Artaxiad linguistic borrowings, which were not limited to vocabulary and included all kinds of names, came from the north-western Iranian language. Even native words, related to social and religious vocabularies, were later replaced by words borrowed from the Parthians.

# CHAPTER 3

Tigranes loved truthful servants, holding them in high regard. He conducted fair trials and executed anyone who betrayed him. All his actions were directed to the benefit of his state, rather than achieving glory and popularity in society. He established a new order throughout the territory and issued his first coins, to commemorate his coronation. These depicted his royal headgear in profile, looking to the right. It took him a year to create a standing army of 35,000 soldiers, including infantrymen, cavalrymen (cataphracts) and mounted archers, strengthened by a force of chariots – all commonly used in the Persian and Seleucid armies.

The backbone of Tigranes' army in the initial stage of his reign consisted of Armenians. Based on the military experience he gained from the Parthians, he made foot soldiers, composed of the peasant classes, into horsemen, and slingers into skilful archers. The latter was suitable for skirmishes and hit-and-run tactics. The cataphracts, equipped with long lances, wore steel helmets, a coat of mail reaching to the knees, covered with steel that enabled them to resist strong bows. He then united all the military forces into the royal army, turning it into a highly organized war machine. Members of the armed guard from the elite class were assigned to the royal palace for the personal protection of the king at all times, and for the surveillance of the royal domains in the close vicinity.

Prior to embarking on his campaigns, the mounted king delivered his first speech to his troops, without revealing his military plans: 'My fellow soldiers, you are this day assembled to celebrate the first standing army ever built in our history. You are also here to confirm the bond of union which ties you to me, and me to you, and both to the Artaxiad dynasty. Our kingdom still stands, despite its misfortunes over the years, and I, from the throne of my ancestors, will continue the legacy they began, and ensure our survival as a nation to become great.' After a pause he continued firmly, 'Everyone in this army is important and plays a vital role. So we shall defend to the death our native land and fight together with confidence and strength. We shall not admit defeat, or contemplate surrender. May obedience to the law, and reverence to the king, be your witness to me and the country.'

Fists raised, the Armenian soldiers, who had listened intently, supported him with loud shouts of joy: 'Long live the King!'

In 94 BC, Tigranes launched his first military campaign, against the adjacent south-western Kingdom of Sophene (east of the upper Euphrates River) and his troops deposed Artanes, the last king from the race of Zariadres, without resistance. Sophene was part of the ancient Kingdom of Ararat (Urartu) in the eighth and seventh centuries BC. Around the third century BC, the Seleucid Empire forced

Sophene to split from Greater Armenia, giving rise to the Kingdom of Sophene – ruled by a branch of the Iranian Orontids - with its capital Carcathiocerta, located north of modern-day Diyarbekir. As Iranian cults were popular at the time, the nobility gave themselves Iranian names and the peasantry regularly sacrificed horses and cows in honour of the goddess Anahita.

From the beginning of the second century BC, Zariadres and Artaxias, two former generals of the Seleucid King Antiochus III the Great, after his defeat, had begun to reign with Roman consent as independent kings – the first one of Sophene, the other of Artaxata. King Tigranes, who had a rightful dynastic claim to these thrones, continued the legacy of his predecessors – the creators of historical Armenia – and put the kingdom back under the control of Greater Armenia. He then assigned aristocratic families high positions, as they expected him to do. Thus, as an immediate show of his power, he reunited the two Armenian regions politically. From this point on, with the exception of a few short intervals, Sophene remained part of Greater Armenia.

# CHAPTER 4

In 119 BC, Mithridates VI, fifteen-year-old Eupator Dionysius and the last King of Pontus, inherited from his father (Mithridates V) a wealthy, multi-ethnic Black Sea kingdom. It stretched across much of the eastern half of the southern shores of the Black Sea, across Armenia Minor – a territory under the king's jurisdiction – and bordered the rugged highlands of Armenia Major (Greater Armenia) in the east. On coming to the throne, the new young king recruited ethnically diverse large armies from distant lands, with the aim of having a powerful Black Sea empire and rivalling Rome's might.

In the following years, Mithridates first subjugated Colchis (modern-day Georgia), rapidly followed by the annexation of Crimea, Tauric Chersonesus, and the Bosporian kingdom. The Scythians were a dominant force in the Crimean Peninsula region at that time. They were the ancient archenemies of the Greeks of Chersonesos Taurica and the Cimmerian Bosporus. The loss of their independence allowed the Pontic king to enlarge his kingdom, which extended in the shape of a serpent to the northern half shores of the Black Sea. Those several campaigns against the Scythians were carried out by his competent general, Diophantus of Sinope, who cleverly used a combination of force and diplomacy. Turning his attention to the west of Anatolia, where Roman power was on the rise, with King Nicomedes III of Bithynia, Mithridates somehow contrived to partition Paphlagonia and Galatia, but Nicomedes soon changed course and deserted the Pontic king, for fear of Roman retribution.

Proud of his harmoniously combined Achaemenid and Macedonian heritages, Mithridates possessed the intellectual capacity to speak numerous tribal languages, with no need of an interpreter. He claimed descent, on his father's side, from Cyrus and Darius the Great, and, on his mother's side, from Alexander the Great, adopting the frizzy, flowing hairstyle and fierce gaze of the latter. After the defeat of the Scythians by the Pontic king, who thus protected the Black Sea Greeks and their cities from the enemies, his reputation as a benefactor of the Greek world had significantly increased. Like the Macedonian king, he became a great protector of Greek civilization, and intended to use this stance (Hellenism) as a political tool in his future clashes with Rome.

Mithridates' entourage described him as a man of extraordinary physical strength, wearing a purple cloak with a bronze Phrygian helmet, carrying an ornate sword, and holding a sceptre on ceremonial occasions. After one hunt, Mithridates had the carcass of a slain lion brought to his capital city, Sinope, and had the animal's head skinned. To imitate Heracles (the son of Zeus and divine hero), he wore the lion pelt, which rested atop his head like a hood or headdress, paws draped down on either side.

Since Hannibal and Pyrrhus of Epirus, the Pontic king was the new most persistent enemy of Rome, which he saw as a continuous force of evil, treachery and deceit. Known as a vindictive Oriental tyrant, ambitious expansionist, ruthless opportunist and a connoisseur of poison, he was also a man of indomitable spirit, even in his misfortunes. While he concerned himself solely with consolidating his own power, and divided his kingdom into satrapies, he extended his great dislike of the Romans as "barbarians" to the western Anatolian population. As a result, a large portion of the populace approved of the King of Pontus.

However, Mithridates was now seeking a strong, dependable alliance on the eastern flank of his domains, to reduce his concerns if he decided to attack the Roman provinces in western Asia Minor. He particularly aspired to the annexation of Cappadocia (east-central Asia Minor) – to which he had at least some territorial claim. For his own reasons, he mostly stressed his father's claim to the territory. The eldest child and daughter of Mithridates V, Laodice of Cappadocia, had married – through an arranged marriage – the King of Cappadocia, Ariarathes VI, who seized the throne back in 130 BC.

Although the Pontic king was wondering if a limited aggression there would be thwarted by Rome, he kept trying to balance the realities that an independent king like himself must face when confronted by a superior power, having enormous resources to draw on. He did not dream of riches and fame, but of the very survival of his Greco-Persian-Anatolian ideals, and of freedom from Roman domination.

Mithridates had already been informed by his fellow Parthians of Tigranes' return to Armenia, and his coronation there. Tigranes' initial conquest of Sophene made Mithridates think that it would be a good idea to gain Armenia as an ally. At this time, the Parthian king was also concerned about the growing extent of Rome's power and its possible infringement into Parthian affairs. To repulse further Roman advances in the region, he and his Pontic counterpart decided to choose King Tigranes to support them.

# CHAPTER 5

In 93 BC, the King of Pontus sent his most trusted envoy, Gordius, to Artaxata, where he was ushered into Tigranes' royal court. The envoy bowed then sat on the seat provided for him. He handed Mithridates' letter over to the new king and said courteously, 'Your Majesty, Mithridates – Eupator and King of Pontus – would like to inform you that the Romans have designs on Asia Minor and are intolerant of independent monarchs there.'

'No one doubts Rome's expansionist policy, but I don't see at this stage any danger of its dominance in our region,' Tigranes replied.

'Mithridates and you are targeted to become vassal states of Rome one day. I'm sure you know what that means. So he proposes an alliance, under which you could extend your kingdom freely to the south and east, without interference from his army, but he would have the right to conquer lands from Asia Minor to the west.'

Tigranes thought he would benefit from the alliance. 'I agree,' he said, 'as long as the two of us will respect each other's spheres of influence.'

'Of course, Your Majesty,' Gordius replied firmly. 'This alliance will secure your domains against the threat from the Roman puppet ruler, Ariobarzanes in Cappadocia. But you'd be better off removing him from there.'

Tigranes, having listened carefully to Gordius, knew what the envoy was implying. 'After all,' he said, slightly annoyed, 'my alliance with Mithridates should not require me to become directly involved in his campaigns; just to some extent to protect each other's flanks.'

'You're right,' Gordius said. 'In exchange for the goodwill on your part, Mithridates would like to give his well-educated and beloved daughter, Cleopatra, to you in marriage.'

Tigranes nodded in approval as he had no queen yet. For him, his enthronement and the marriage proposal were not accidental events but well-considered moves made by the Parthian and Pontic kings to fulfil their political aims through his support. Gordius, having made this family attachment and sealed a bond of friendship, bowed to the king and left the palace to report the good news to Mithridates.

In the same year, Tigranes married sixteen-year-old Princess Cleopatra, in the Pontic kingdom. The royal wedding ceremony started with the couple's offerings – a lock of the bride's hair – and a sacrifice to the ancient gods, to bless the two being wed. The two royal families both adhered to the teachings and beliefs of Zoroastrianism and their religion hinged on Mazdaism – the worship of the gods, Ahura Mazda and Mithra. After the wedding, the bride's father held a lavish feast in his great palace, in the presence of family members and other guests. Poetic performances, along with dance and music, in which flutes, lutes and harps were used, featured in such traditional wedding celebrations.

On the following day, a treaty of cooperation and mutual defence was signed, then ratified by the swearing of an oath, which involved both parties, thus cementing the strong alliance between Pontus and Armenia.

Royal intermarriages – a tool of political diplomacy in the Ancient Near East – were designed to cement alliances based on political interests and establish treaties between neighbouring dynastic kingdoms. Local magi priests performed traditional fire ceremonies in temples associated with the creed preached by the prophet Zoroaster (Avesta) – the sacred book of Zoroastrianism. Sacrifices were also offered on mountaintops, in the grand manner of the Persian kings.

In antiquity, it was also common practice for kings to marry their sisters, and for queens to marry their younger brothers. The reason was to keep the royal line pure by preventing other families marrying in. The royal incest set the king above society and sometimes made him become god-like. In Ancient Greece, Spartan King Leonidas I had married his niece, Gorgo, daughter of his half-brother Cleomenes I. Greek law in past times allowed marriage between a brother and sister if they had different mothers. The religious Greek people believed god Zeus had married his sister, the goddess Hera. According to the Hebrew Bible, Sarah was Patriarch Abraham's half-sister and wife.

# CHAPTER 6

Tigranes was a few years older than Mithridates, whose name in old Persian was Mithradatha, meaning "gift of the god Mithra". The two new allies were of imposing physical nature and astonishing energy. They became very close friends, as they had much in common. Both kings kept large harems with appointed eunuchs, and inherited important Persian cultural traditions, mixed with Greek elements. Their courts were structured along Hellenistic lines, to become the centre for Greek and Persian philosophers, poets and the like. The only thing that differentiated the two men was the foreign policy they pursued independently of each other and based on their own individual interests.

They enjoyed riding and hunting together on horseback. For them, the hunt was a royal activity, more than a pleasure or sport. It was something that most of the kings in ancient times were expected to do, to show how they could extend their control even over the wilderness. The obligation to kill animals was a responsibility these Near-Eastern rulers accepted, as their claim to leadership was based precisely on these ventures, including sacrifices of some of their hunted creatures to Ahura Mazda and other important gods in ritual ceremonies.

When Tigranes and Mithridates went hunting, they were dressed in Persian hunter garbs. Equipped with bows, arrows, swords and a long spear, they knew the perfect place to hunt for animals such as jackal, leopard, panther, hawk and falcon, galloping after them at full tilt.

One day, as they rode slowly along a shallow river, exchanging jokes, they were taken aback by a huge lion emerging from the nearby woods. 'We've got company,' Tigranes said.

The animal was keeping its tail stiff, twitching it from time to time.

'I think he's hunting us. Keep still,' Mithridates replied quietly.

But when Tigranes saw the lion approaching them with a roar, he snatched two arrows from his quiver and shot them towards the animal, which yowled in pain as blood gushed from the ensuing wounds.

Not finished, the lion was just about to pounce on Mithridates, who exclaimed, 'Take this from me now,' and forcefully thrust his spear into the lion's throat. Struggling to breathe, the animal collapsed slowly and painfully to its death, in a pool of blood.

'We've killed the bloody beast,' Mithridates boasted and continued after a pause, 'In some of my campaigns against my enemies, I've worn the lion's head skin like a hood, and will continue to do so.'

'Do you wear it for any reason?' Tigranes asked.

'I just want to imitate Heracles.'

Tigranes smiled to himself at his ally's ridiculous imitation and thought he was lucky to have a crown of his own.

Sometimes, both kings stayed at Tigranes' hunting lodges in his mountain estates, during which time they conversed in Greek, though they knew Parthian as well. On one occasion, Mithridates said to his friend, 'When I was still a baby, a lightning bolt struck my cradle, leaving a unique scar in the shape of a crown on my forehead. My birth actually coincided with the first of two significant comets, which blazed forth so brightly that the heavens seemed to be on fire.'

'A fascinating story,' Tigranes said. 'When did it appear?'

'About four decades ago. Its long, shining tail was curved across the sky like a bladed weapon, and it's the reason I was given the nickname "Dionysus".'

'So the divine forces crowned you at birth.'

'Yes. And in the first years of my reign,' Mithridates continued, 'a second comet appeared.'

'I remember having observed one in Parthia in the distant past,' Tigranes recalled.

'That's exactly the same comet that had enabled me to strike my own coins; one with a starburst and the other a horse's head, Pegasus, on one side,' Mithridates said.

'Why did you choose that animal as your own emblem?'

'Because my first comet appeared in the constellation of Pegasus, which represents the white-winged horse of Greek mythology.'

'What about the reverse of the coin?' Tigranes asked, to compare his first coinage with the one of his ally.

'It depicted, amongst other things, a palm branch; a sign of victory and of a saviour king.'

'I assume you'll be that saviour king,' Tigranes said, half-jokingly.

Mithridates laughed, 'You'll see.'

The coming of an oriental saviour king born under an Eastern star loomed in Mithridates' lifetime. His two divine comets, along with the oracles and prophecies, had nurtured the king's long-held ambition to fight against the tyranny of Rome. They would later help him provide the popular backing of his campaigns against the Romans.

# CHAPTER 7

In 93/92 BC, at the instigation of Mithridates, Tigranes' troops, led by his two generals, Bagoas and Mithras, invaded Cappadocia. For the allied kings, this attack was launched as a way of testing the Roman resolve. They dethroned the Roman puppet ruler, Ariobarzanes I – who fled to Rome – and installed the thirteen-year-old son of Mithridates, Ariarathes IX Eusebes Philopator, on the throne, under the guidance of his father's henchman, Gordius. The latter was used as an instrument of Mithridates in his attempts to annex Cappadocia to Pontus. The news was received with some joy by a fraction of the Cappadocians, while the rest favoured the Romans, who had been provided ground for their entry in Asia Minor. Prior to the invasion of the province, the Pontic king had forged another agreement with Tigranes, under which the former would take control of the cities, whereas all captives and treasure – a great quantity of gold and silver – would go to the latter.

In the same year, Rome reacted strongly to a regime change in Cappadocia; something Tigranes failed to foresee. Lucius Cornelius Sulla, propraetor of the Cilician province, came to Asia Minor with an armed force and orders from the Senate. The Roman commander drove Mithridates' candidate from the Cappadocian throne and reinstated the legitimate ruler, Ariobarzanes. Tigranes' first encounter with Rome was inconclusive but the Pontic king waited for the right moment to regain his dominant position in Cappadocia.

By this time, Rome had already formed a "Province of Asia" in Asia Minor, which paved the way for a meeting between Sulla and the Parthian ambassador Orobaze. However, the King of Parthia wisely refused to agree to follow the Roman path and preferred to retain his neutrality in the struggle between Rome and the Pontic king. Eventually, they forged an agreement, which set the Roman-Persian frontier on the Euphrates River.

In 91 BC, the level of tension in Rome was raised, with the uprising of the Italian tribes. The reason for this unstable political situation was the refusal of the Senate to grant Roman citizenship to the Socii, old Italian allies, as well as a demand for more respect and better treatment of the Latin subjects, who remained as a whole loyal to Rome. The plans of the allies were at an advanced stage by this point, and the Romans, suspecting something was in the air, sent out envoys to the various allied towns in vain.

Masri, Peligni, Vestini and Marrucini declared war, which placed the revolt close to Rome. While the four allied rebels took the revolt across to the Adriatic coast, next to declare war were the Picentines to the north and a large group of tribes to the south. Among them were the Frentani, the Hirpini, the Venusini and the Samnites. The

Italian rebels succeeded in mobilizing their forces of about 100,000 men, while the Romans had their Latin allies and those loyal Italian allies.

Tigranes and Mithridates were informed of Rome's internal dissensions by their agents. Taking advantage of the situation there, the Pontic king sent his son, Ariarathes, into Cappadocia with a strong army and had the same Roman puppet ruler, Ariobarzanes, ousted again from his throne and the rule of the Pontic son reinforced.

In 89 BC, the Roman commander Manius Aquillius came as ambassador to Asia Minor and restored Nicomedes IV, Bithynia's puppet king, who had been recently expelled from his kingdom by Mithridates. After that, Aquillius left the retaliatory raid against Pontus to Nicomedes without Senate authorization. This prompted a furious backlash from Mithridates, which marked the first stages of his first direct war against the Roman provinces. He quickly built an even larger army, of 95,000 horsemen, and placed his general, Archelaus, in command. With the aid of Tigranes' 6000 cavalrymen, the Pontic troops marched back to the west. The Roman republic saw such an alliance between the two regional Oriental monarchs and their joint campaign as a direct challenge to its vital interests in Asia Minor.

In the meantime, Aquillius and his ally were defeated, and retreated after thousands of their men were killed and more than 300 prisoners captured. The Roman commander, attempting to escape back to Italy, managed to make it to Lesbos, where he was delivered to Mithridates by the inhabitants of Mytilene. Aquillius was tied to a donkey and paraded through the region. After he was forced to confess his crimes against the peoples of Anatolia, Mithridates had him executed.

Back in 90 BC, Rome's continuous intransigence of the civil liberties of its enemies triggered the Italian Social War. Following the defeat of the Roman armies by the Socii in the north and the south of the country, Consul Lucius Julius Caesar felt compelled to make concessions by granting Roman citizenship, first to the Italians who were not engaged in the Social War, and then to the rebels, if they laid down their arms. The Romans believed that everything was controlled by the power of ancient gods – Jupiter, Juno, Mars – with whom they almost constantly communicated. Under favourable circumstances, they held sacrifices and gave thanks to them, or tried to appease their tempers otherwise.

# CHAPTER 8

Around 88 BC, the aged King Mithridates II of Parthia died. As a result, his whole empire weakened, due to internal dissensions and invasions by the Scythians. These domestic troubles made the king's loss more sensibly felt by his supporters. Tigranes, who had foreseen the political turmoil, no longer wanted to rule as a mere puppet of Parthia. The reason he had waited for so long to act was the respect he had developed for the Parthian king during and after his hostage years. Moreover, one of Tigranes' daughters, Aryazate, surnamed Automa and born to a Persian woman, was the wife of the new Parthian monarch Gotarzes I – the son and successor of Mithridates II.

Seven years after his return to Artaxata, Tigranes was now ready to recapture the lands he had once ceded to the Parthians, in order to gain the trust of his people. He underlined his determination to expand his kingdom to its furthest reaches, to one day become the strongest nation in the East. One key motivating factor in his expansionist policy was his treaty of alliance with the Pontic king, which gave Tigranes the momentum he needed to establish his position as a powerful leader in the region. Taking advantage of the conflicts in Parthia, Tigranes' troops invaded the south-eastern provinces and re-conquered the seventy valleys that had been a bone of contention between Armenia and Parthia for a long time.

The king then turned his attention to Mesopotamia, meaning "between the rivers" and known as the "Cradle of Civilization" for the many valuable innovations that had emerged from the earlier societies in this region. These peoples included the Sumerians, Assyrians, Akkadians, and Babylonians. However, Mesopotamia was once the site of constant internal conflicts. It was prey to continual disputes over resources, and open to attack from outside invaders. As early as the middle of the second century BC, the local dynasts had enjoyed a period of independence, until about 124 BC when Mesopotamia was in Parthian hands.

Within a year or so, following his own political agenda, Tigranes annexed into his kingdom the northern Mesopotamian neighbouring dynastic states of Media Atropatene, Gordyene, Adiabene – with the important centre of Arbela – and Osrhoene (Edessa). While the Parthians were dealing with the invading nomads, Tigranes' forces pushed as far as the gates of Ecbatana, where they burned down the royal palace at Adrapana on the great road to the west of Ecbatana and sacked the Parthian court's summer residence. Although all those principalities became the vassals of Tigranes but kept their political apparatus, they were obliged to pay tribute to his victorious army.

On 6th August 87 BC, Tigranes had seen the later-named Halley's Comet when it passed closest to the sun. This was the most significant and recordable event in the Near East and his life, heralding the new era of the rise of a powerful king. Comets had been described by Greco-Romans as bad omens, and the one that appeared during this period had sent tremors through their countries. But the populations of Anatolia and of the old Persian Empire interpreted comets as a sign of success. So Tigranes declared to his subjects that he did not fear them and would like to embrace the comet, wearing it on his tiara as a symbol throughout his reign.

In 85 BC, the Parthians officially recognized Tigranes as the supreme ruler of the East. In fact, Tigranes' acceptance of the revelation of the divine comet two years earlier became now an astonishing reality. It proved very beneficial to him, as he took the proud old Achaemenid title of "King of Kings" (Shahanshah), which later appeared on his coins. The other coins depicted the comet star on his crown having a long, curved tail. The appearance of Tigranes' first comet was also an important sign of his strong alliance and friendship with Mithridates so far.

By this time, the northern two Caucasian Kingdoms of Iberia (present-day Georgia) and Albania (present-day Azerbaijan) both divided into many different tribes and languages, were forced to defend themselves against foreign invasions into their territories. For one, was the defence of the passes of Caucasus against various tribes migrating west and southwards from the steppes of Central Asia. Taking advantage of the situation there, Tigranes expanded his domains at the expense of Albania, which he subjected to his authority. Although it maintained a measure of autonomy and its own royal dynasty, the Albanians pledged their loyalty and support to him.

As for the Kingdom of Iberia, it was already under the rule of the Artaxiads, who had acquired its crown, following a revolt of Iberian nobles against their king, Pharnajom. During a great battle between a combined Iberian-Artaxiad army and the king backed by his followers, the latter was heavily defeated and killed, after which a prince named Arshak of the Artaxiad dynasty became the King of Iberia.

During Tigranes' expeditions, four satrap-kinglets, who served him as attendants or close counsellors, followed him everywhere; two on each side of his horse. Throughout the audiences given by the king to ambassadors, they always stood submissively to attention on both sides of his throne. Tigranes kept his military plans a secret from his entourage and only shared confidences with his most trusted generals, whom he sent forth to lead his armies, although he rarely took direct part in war himself. These generals were informed about their king's strategy, focused on twin goals: to convince the enemy that ongoing war against his army was more costly than submitting, and making the most gain possible from war.

# CHAPTER 9

The one source of Tigranes' power and wisdom was his unusual obsession with waterfalls. Every time he was marching his army back from foreign land to his dominion, he always chose the long route so as to incorporate the largest waterfalls, in which he would jump and bathe for a long time. His soldiers had to wait until he had finished. After praying at the nearby temple of Zeus as a tribute to his first victories, he would then return to his palace, well refreshed and rejuvenated. Even people close to him never asked him about this strange waterfall habit, thinking that it was just a whim of their king. Others thought his visit to the falls was meant to dispel languor and raise spirits.

One day, one of his loyal servants, driven by curiosity, came to him and summoned the courage to ask, 'If His Majesty pleases, could he perhaps say something about his interest in waterfalls?'

'I don't like to explain things that do not require any explanation,' Tigranes said bluntly, but then relented and asked, 'If I tell you a secret, do you promise to keep it?'

'Yes, Your Majesty,' the servant replied firmly.

'I always bathe in waterfalls so that the foreign dust upon me may be washed away and I may feel the spirit of my ancestors. The magic water in Armenia gives me strength and power for new battles ahead.'

'Has it really given you that power, Your Majesty?'

'Absolutely. My victories are sufficient proof, are they not?'

The servant nodded and walked away.

While Tigranes expanded his political sphere of influence on the neighbouring dynastic states of Mesopotamia and northern Caucasian regions, Mithridates had taken advantage of the Roman political strife and invaded nearby territories, including Bithynia, which marked the outbreak of the First Mithridatic War, back in 89 BC. The Eupator of Pontus had demonstrated his resolve by conquering within weeks all of Rome's possessions, encountering hardly any resistance. So many fortunes invested in the provinces by Romans of all orders were completely lost. They realized they would be in very bad trouble financially if they did not reclaim Asia Minor.

Meanwhile, the king was hailed as a god in the region. After Oracles promised him victory, and on the advice of the prominent Greek philosopher at his court, Metrodorus of Scepsis – a Roman-hater – he had ordered the execution without mercy of every Roman and Italian man, woman and child in Asia Minor. 'I will kill them all,' he shouted, and more than 80,000 were massacred in cold blood in one day as he captured Roman cities. The massacre came to be known as the Asiatic Vespers.

Mithridates had then given his general, Archelaus, the command of his large navy and army to lead them into

Greece, to liberate the country from long Roman rule. On their way to Athens, the general captured the many Cyclades islands in the Aegean Sea and the island of Delos. The king envisioned a united Greece under his banner, which was a big threat to Rome's interests in that region. He was hailed by the demoralized Greeks as a liberator and hero, for they had bad memories of the Romans, who had brought much suffering and systematically enslaved the entire population of Athens. In their vandalisms, they had completely destroyed the ancient city of Corinth back in 146 BC – a great tragedy never forgotten by the Greeks. Since then, the Greek peninsula had become a Roman protectorate.

In 88 BC, Consul Lucius Sulla was placed in command of the war against Mithridates VI. As the new Roman general was gathering strength on his move, the Roman governor of Macedonia, Sentius, granted him full control of the campaign. In the following year, Sulla marched with five legions against Athens and its main port, Piraeus, to recover southern Greece and avenge the massacre of Roman citizens by Mithridates. At that time, Athens was ruled by Aristion, the Athenian tyrant and Mithridates' puppet. Sulla first faced heavy resistance from the Pontic forces under the command of Archelaus. Besieged in the city, where its population was starving and reduced to eating grass, the general desperately continued to break the siege, until the city had fallen to Sulla's forces in 86 BC and was sacked at midnight.

Archelaus quickly withdrew to Macedonia and, after joining the new Mithridates' army, moved south once again to face Sulla. The army of 120,000 soldiers, commanded now by Taxiles, another of Mithridates' generals, outnumbered Sulla's forces three to one. He marched towards Chaeronea and positioned himself on high ground, while Sulla occupied the ruined city of Parapotamii, which was impregnable. Archelaus tried to outflank Sulla's men, but in a clever military strategy the latter broke the enemy's flank continually and caused great confusion and damage in its army, resulting in heavy casualties. Archelaus then managed to escape with only 10,000 men.

The government of Rome sent out Flaccus with an additional Roman army to counter Mithridates. As for Archelaus, he recruited again a new army of 150,000 and crossed back into Boeotia. Sulla moved to intercept the Pontic army at Orchomenus – a town he chose for the battle to come and an ideal terrain for his use of entrenchment. Archelaus encamped in front of the Roman army at a nearby lake, while Sulla's soldiers had been digging trenches, and before long they had the Pontic army in deep trouble. Hurled at the Romans, the battle turned into a slaughter on a large scale and the Roman legionnaires routed the enemy's army. Sulla had eventually reclaimed southern Greece, thus putting an end to the invasion of its peninsula by Mithridates.

Since Sulla had to return to Rome to deal with its Social War, he had concluded in the summer of 85 BC a lenient peace treaty with Mithridates, at the Peace of Dardanos. It stipulated that Mithridates had to surrender a part of his fleet, abandon claims to all lands outside of Pontus – a return to pre-war status quo – and pay a moderate indemnity of a mere 2,000 talents. Sulla's legions had complained that the Pontic king got off lightly. Eventually, Ariobarzanes of Cappadocia and Nicomedes IV of Bithynia had been restored. Although Tigranes' kingdom remained neutral and Mithridates, financially supported by the Parthians, had started his first war successfully, the outcome was disappointing and his long-awaited dream of a saviour king proved illusory.

Rome was unprepared for this war, as a result of the long civil conflicts at home on the one hand, and on the other the economic problems and lack of funds to keep enough of its troops in the occupied provinces. However, Mithridates learned from his agents that the peace afforded by these domestic dissensions was only a postponement of the struggle between him and the Romans. The war, cruel and devastating, in which many cities were on the brink of collapse and there was much looting on both sides, had ended within the year, with Roman control over Asia Minor once more.

# CHAPTER 10

In 83 BC, a bloody strife for the throne of Syria, governed by the Seleucid princes, tore the nation apart. The populace became weary of the endless Seleucid dynastic quarrels. By this time, the Seleucids reigned from Antioch and refused to accept Philip I's minor son, Philip II, as his successor. Under the pretext of putting an end to these civil contests, Tigranes' armies marched into the area. This inevitably faced some resistance to Tigranes' rule, from the faction of the local aristocracy. Following the defeat of the Seleucid king Antiochus Eusebes, the majority of Syrians, tired of continuous anarchy, chose Tigranes as the protector of their kingdom and offered him the crown of Syria. The new conqueror then removed the southern tent-dwelling Arabs from their habitual haunts and transferred them to an adjacent settlement to employ them in trade and commerce.

After the fall of the Seleucid kingdom, Tigranes seized the remaining Seleucid domains in Cilicia Pedias and sacked Soli, a coastal port-city. Numerous cities were established, which minted various coins, depicting the badges – animals, gods, objects – associated with each polis. He then subdued the neighbouring Kingdom of Commagene – an ancient Greco-Iranian kingdom ruled by a Hellenized branch of the Iranian Orontid dynasty. Their successive kings claimed descent from Orontes with Darius I of Persia as their ancestor. Tigranes' forces then marched further south and conquered Antioch, where the mass of population was Hellenic and the spoken language Aramaic in non-official life. Tigranes appointed one of his generals, Magadates, as his governor, to command most of Syria, which would enjoy peace for about fourteen years.

The king prayed at the Hellenized temple of Zeus in Antioch as a tribute to his latest victories. In the following years of the domination of Syria, Tigranes forced the population of the lands that he captured, to move to his eastern domains, where he had in mind to build his new capital and transplant them there. During the hundreds of kilometres long walk, one part of these people had died of starvation, thirst and exposure. The Greek element of the country's population detested the rule of Tigranes, who had become pompous during his great prosperity. For them, he seemed to be aiming to become the successor to King Xerxes I the Great, the fifth King of Kings of the earlier Achaemenid dynasty of Persia. Meanwhile, the Romans portrayed him as an alien, imperious Oriental monarch, and his army as barbarian hordes.

To commemorate the capture of Antioch, which became temporarily his main residence in the south, the monarch re-issued magnificent coins in its minting centre, as well as in Damascus. This helped Tigranes cope with the growing needs of commercial transactions and the demands of his varying army payments. The silver and copper coins, the latter used within his domains, bore an image of his head in profile, looking to the right and wearing his pearl-pointed crown with the starburst between two eagles. The emblems on the two coins were almost the same. The reverse of these coins depicted the effigy of goddess Tyche, represented in the customary Hellenistic fashion as a seated woman on a rock or a throne, wearing a turreted crown and holding the palm branch of victory. The reverse of other coins bore engravings depicting images of fire, temples and the like.

Tigranes' kingdom had been divided into three major estates, or viceroyalties, administered locally: those of the nakharars (lords), who were the real owners and masters of the land; those of the lesser nobility, Azats (freemen) – the most numerous members of the aristocracy – as well as the elite forces of the army, and members of the king's guard. The third estate consisted of the artisans and peasants.

During this period, Tigranes embarked on a large project to build his dream capital city of Tigranocerta, to commemorate the creation of Greater Armenia. It was customary for kings in ancient times to name their cities after themselves. The king considered the old capital of Artaxata too far north, and isolated from the major ancient trade routes. He envisioned the new capital, to be built with the accumulated treasures of conquered lands, full of grandeur – a fortress surrounded by high and mighty walls, acting as a formidable bulwark against invader entry. He aimed to make the city one of the seven wonders of the Ancient Near East. It would serve as a symbol of greatness and glory for his victorious campaigns. Designed to reflect the mixed heritage of his kingdom with Greek and Persian elements, it would also become one of the centres of Hellenistic culture and civilization.

The location of the city was to be chosen by master architects, after exact calculations and planning. They had to take into account the lines of alignment on the crossroads of the important trade routes of the ancient world. One such road was the Persian Royal road, connecting East to West. Thus, the architects began searching for a strategically important location that would fulfil the multi-dimensional requirements of such an ambitious endeavour.

# CHAPTER 11

When Sulla withdrew from Asia Minor to return to a politically fractured Rome back in 85 BC, he left Lucius Murena, his governor of Asia, in charge of keeping the province stable. The Roman leaders kept a low profile regarding internal rivals, to maintain their dominance over foreign foes. Murena soon heard rumours that Mithridates had been building up a new army for an expedition across the Black Sea, to deal with a rebellion in his northern territories. Hoping to win a remarkable triumph for himself, the ambitious Murena carried out two raids into Pontic territory, without Senate approval, and without considering a military response.

After ignoring further orders from the Senate to stop operations there, he launched a third raid, in 82 BC. Mithridates reacted quickly and sent an army under the Cappadocian Pontic general, Gordius, to oppose Murena. The two armies came face-to-face across the Halys River, and when Mithridates came in person with his own army, the combined Pontic forces attacked the Roman positions and made them suffer a crushing defeat. Mithridates sent an envoy to Murena to invoke the peace treaty, but the latter replied that he did not see any treaties. The Pontic king then sent envoys to Rome to complain, after which Sulla's envoy, Aulus Gabinius, arrived in Asia Minor and ordered the governor to withdraw immediately. He then reinstated the peace treaty between Pontus and the Roman provinces. The Second Mithridatic War (83-81 BC) ended without any significant territorial gains for either side, resulting in the transfer of a strip of Cappadocia to Pontic control.

Given that the royal intrigues against kings were commonplace in the Ancient East, Mithridates worried that he could be the target of homicidal plots. During that period, political dinner table poisonings in foods and drinks were the preferred method of kings, queens, every social class, and even the nobility, who wished to dispose of unwanted political opponents. With assassination, betrayal and backstabbing on a constant basis, Mithridates started feeling paranoid about somebody poisoning him. He refused to hire a taster to test his food or drink for poison at all times. Instead, he accustomed himself to various poisons to become immune.

His father, King Mithridates V, was assassinated in Sinope (capital of Pontus) in 120 BC, poisoned by unknown persons during a feast in the castle. Since then, his mother, Laodice VI, had retained all power as regent, for both her sons were too young to rule. But during her regency she favoured her second son, Chrestus, for the Pontic throne. Mithridates, a minor at the time and fearing for his own life, had escaped from the plotting of his mother and gone into long-term hiding. The major trauma of his father's death by poison had shaped the young Mithridates' life, compelling him to work on medical research, which paved the way for a good knowledge of the immune system, herbalism, and antidotes.

On his return to Pontus, back in 115 BC, he had grown up to become a man of considerable stature and physical strength, with a considerable talent for political strategy and organization. The young Mithridates had his mother and brother, Chrestus, thrown into prison, where they both died. After giving them royal funerals, he married his sixteen-year-old sister, Laodice. Mithridates' main goal was to preserve the purity of their bloodline, solidify his claim to the throne, and to ensure the succession to his children. Thus, he was hailed as the new Pontic ruler.

On one occasion, around 79 BC, at Mithridates' request, he and Tigranes met at the border of their kingdoms, to renew their alliance. The Pontic king discussed with his ally the latest developments in his second war with Rome. He told him about the peace treaty Sulla had once concluded with him at the Peace of Dardanos and how everything ended. He then re-expressed his long-standing concern about homicidal plots in his domains. He said that during his first war with the Romans, some of his friends – Mynnio and Philotimus of Smyrna – plotted to kill him. The conspirators were tortured and executed, and all the plotters' families and friends killed. Since then, he had trusted no one, and always ensured that he would be safe not only from assassination but also from poison.

Tigranes was astounded to learn that as a youngster Mithridates had started a complex, rigid programme to educate himself about every form of poison, conducting later experiments on different formulations and testing their effectiveness on condemned prisoners. Mithridates eventually succeeded in compounding various antidotes to produce a single one. After that, he had fortified his body with this antidote – an invented secret potion – and consumed it daily in small doses, building in himself an immunity and resistance to being poisoned.

When Tigranes asked why that knowledge was being kept secret, his ally said many others would wish to steal the poison-recipe from him. He added that when his guards left at midnight he was protected while he slept by his horse, standing outside the palace, which would whinny a warning if anybody should try to sneak up on him.

# CHAPTER 12

In 78 BC, the fortress city of Tigranocerta, its construction not yet complete, was being built on the very soil that formerly belonged to the Parthians. The Batman River – a tributary of the Tigris – entered the city through its northern bank. The king had employed Greeks and a huge number of captives, once taken from Cappadocia, to construct the city, which was located east of present-day Diyarbakir. Hellenistic in its architecture, the metropolis reflected the mixed cultural heritage of Greece and Persia, combined with Armenian elements. It was safely protected by the steep slopes on the north and the royal road of the Achaemenids on the south, thus connecting the important trading routes and centres of the kingdom to the capital.

The city, where Tigranes had accumulated all his wealth, inaugurated another mint. The site had impressive fortifications with huge walls fifty cubits (300 feet) high, from which several towers were projected on either side. Stables were built into the lower, larger, ramparts of the walls, to be used for storage rooms; warehouses for ammunition, armaments, and food supplies. The royal palace, along with large parks, magnificent gardens, and hunting grounds, were in the suburbs, outside the city walls – an architecture on an imperial scale of Persian type, thought to have rivalled Babylon. Fire temples and Zoroastrian fire altars were erected, in honour of Ahura Mazda, in the outskirts of Tigranocerta and in various parts of the king's domains. Tigranes' many vassal states properly paid their taxes and the city began to prosper.

In the meantime, the monarch was determined to populate his new royal city, to which he forcibly transplanted the inhabitants of the once devastated regions of Cappadocia, Adiabene, Gordyene, and Assyria (300,000 in all). This method of forcible transfer of populations was common in antiquity, to serve the king's programme of reform and national development. Forced resettlement was mainly conducted for the economic and cultural benefit of the states or empires, and not necessarily meant to provide a better future for the deportees.

Tigranes encouraged the local store managers to produce garments and brocades of various colours for the low-class men and women so as the ugly appeared as wonderful as the handsome. He later brought craftsmen and labourers to enhance the flavour of the city. Traders and merchants filled the capital's markets, which became a great commercial and cultural centre of the Near East. The Arabian nomadic tribes in the king's domains were assigned to guard the trade routes along the southern border, and to charge custom tolls. The imperial treasury had grown to unprecedented proportions, and all Tigranes' wealth was kept in fortified repositories. The new economic boom and the recent introduction of the national coinage strengthened the monarch's position, at the expense of lords and old tribal structures.

The king continued to promote the spread of Hellenism in his domains and designated himself "Philhellene", in imitation of the Parthian kings. Hellenistic culture had been initiated by Alexander the Great three centuries earlier and had taken root throughout the Near East. Greek philosophers, rhetoricians and historians like Amphicrates and Metrodorus were invited to share their ideas at Tigranes' court, which was constructed along the lines of the Achaemenids, with Philhellenic features. The Greek, Persian and Aramaic languages were used by the nobility and administration, while commoners spoke only Greek. A magnificent amphitheatre was built in Hellenistic style, where many guests from the Iranian and Artaxiad Houses attended outdoor dramas and comedies performed by Greek and Armenian actors. One of Tigranes' sons, Artavasdes II, joined the group theatre. A very cultured prince with a mastery of Greek language, he wrote discourses, tragedies, and historical treatises.

One of the performances given was of *Alcestis* – a tragedy by the ancient Greek playwright Euripides, which captivated the audience. Alcestis is the queen of Thessaly and wife of King Admetus of Pherae. When the death of the latter is imminent, his friend Apollo tricks the Fates into allowing Admetus to live if someone else should voluntarily take his place. But no one is willing to sacrifice themselves for the king, except his wife Alcestis, who now on her death-bed entreats her husband never to remarry after her death – never to allow a vicious and resentful stepmother to take charge of their children. Admetus, in return for his wife's sacrifice, promises to live a life with dignity in her honour and abstain from the usual celebrations of his household. The beloved queen then dies and is deeply mourned by everyone in Thessaly.

The Greek hero, Heracles, arrives at the palace, not knowing the queen has died. In order not to burden Heracles with the sad news, Admetus welcomes him with his usual lavish reception, thus breaking his promise to his wife. When Heracles learns of Alcestis' fate, he resolves to fight Thanatos himself, in order to save her and bring the region back to happiness and prosperity. The hero then returns to the palace with a veiled woman whom he gives to Admetus as a new wife. But the king declares he cannot violate his memory of Alcestis by accepting another woman in his life. Finally, after submitting to his old friend's wishes, he finds out that it is in fact Alcestis herself, back from the dead.

# CHAPTER 13

Tigranes' goal was to keep peace within his kingdom, but he was not fully confident that the feudal nobility's loyalty toward their king was always undivided. He feared domestic dissensions would create an atmosphere of political uncertainty. He suspected that some nakharars, who sought to preserve their traditional independence and freedom of action, were trying to deliberately weaken the stability of his monarchy. Secondly, there was a risk that the growing power of the slave-owning nobility could result in conflicts between social classes. Thirdly, he hoped he would not face any revolts by his own sons to seize the throne.

Most importantly, the king had to ensure through his agents that the peoples from conquered provinces, whom he had forcibly settled in the city, would not be manipulated by the neighbouring feudal states or outside forces to bring about political instability in his country. But he was not sure that the granting of land to these peoples, which constituted the basis of royal power, would not affect the interests of the free communal peasants to the point of themselves creating disturbances within the society.

When Sulla died in 78 BC, the short-term peace that he had maintained in Asia Minor began to crumble. Lucius Lucullus, a stateman and Sulla's most trusted associate, took up his command in the East in 74 BC. Meanwhile, Mithridates, in order to fend off Roman aggression, actively cooperated with the Cilician pirates, Thracian tribes and their gladiator, Spartacus, to seek assistance. He then built a massive army to start a new campaign and expand his borders. After learning that Nicomedes IV bequeathed his kingdom to Rome upon his death in 74 BC, the Pontic king was back on route to re-invade the Roman province of Bithynia. This triggered the Third Mithridatic War in the spring of the following year, nearly a decade after the Second Mithridatic War, to last a further ten years of bloody cat-and-mouse conflicts. Speeches were made in the Senate, calling the Pontic king a continuous existential threat to Rome's existence.

Mithridates defeated the Roman consul Marcus Cotta and destroyed his fleet, in a combined land-and-sea battle at Chalcedon (south of the Asian shore of the Bosporus). He then moved west to capture the city of Cyzicus, to use as a supply base for his army, but Lucullus arrived in the region with five legions and aimed to stop the Pontic advance. They went quickly on the offensive and scored a major victory at the battle of Rhyndacus, near the port city of Cyzicus, which was under siege by Mithridates' army. By the time the King of Pontus had abandoned his hopes of conquering the city, he had lost the majority of his soldiers and fled back to Pontus.

Marcus Marius, along with Mithridates' admirals Alexandros and Dionysios, was placed in joint command of fifty ships and 8000 handpicked men. When they sailed east into the Aegean, Lucullus mounted an attack against them and captured a detachment of thirteen ships. As a result, the Pontic force had drawn their ships to shore at the small island of Neae, where the Roman general eventually sunk about thirty ships of the royal fleet supplied by Mithridates. While Dionysios committed suicide, Alexandros was captured and held in captivity for Lucullus' triumph. As for Marius, he escaped and was later found in a cave ashore.

Throughout the conflict, Tigranes maintained his neutrality towards Rome, despite appeals from Cleopatra to save her father. The latter then requested aid from the Parthian King Sanatruces, who also refused to help him. Meanwhile, the Roman general pursued Mithridates and eventually invaded Pontus, where he first besieged several cities. A supply convoy of ten cohorts of infantry under the legate Sornatius was attacked by the Pontic cavalry, but the Romans held off the attack, inflicting heavy losses on the Pontic soldiers. With the Romans re-supplied and Mithridates' forces destroyed, the Pontic king was forced to retreat.

The Roman general then conquered all the cities, including the capital, Sinope, despite the dogged loyalty to the Pontic king from the defenders of the cities. After being defeated in several battles, including the battle of Cabira, Mithridates fled eastward with only 2000 cavalrymen, to the neighbouring territory of Armenia, in 72/71 BC. He did not count on Tigranes to provide shelter, nor did he believe that his ally would damage his public image by abandoning his father-in-law to his fate or turning him over to the Romans. However, he continued to gamble his hope on family ties and on his own salvation.

Following the fall of Mithridates' last stronghold, the

Roman troops looted the enemy camp, but the royal treasures stored at Cabira were reserved for Lucullus. The Roman general went on to invade Armenia Minor, which had been under the influence of the Pontic king.

# CHAPTER 14

Tigranes reluctantly accepted his defeated ally's request for asylum and kept him as a sort of prisoner in a remote old castle, twenty miles away from Tigranocerta. A personal armed bodyguard was assigned to him day and night and all the necessary hospitality provided – food, drink and clothes – according to the teachings of Zoroastrianism. He did not go to visit him, nor did he feel the need to give him any explanation for having stayed out of his devastating last war. However, Mithridates, even in his misfortunes, was a pugnacious leader, determined to take revenge on the Romans.

Cleopatra had a brief argument with her husband in their royal bedchamber one night. 'I think you didn't adequately back my father on his three wars with the Romans. The last one proved to be a humiliating defeat for him,' she said.

'I couldn't commit myself at this stage to supplying him with extra troops,' Tigranes replied.

'Why not?'

'Because my forces, as you probably know, are already stretched too thin throughout my domains. They also need to safeguard the southern border with Parthia on one hand

and against the attacks by the northern tribes on the other.'

'You forged an alliance with my father,' Cleopatra reminded her husband, 'and a treaty of mutual defence and support was signed after our marriage, remember?'

'Yes, but I've already carried out my part of the bargain, and it's not in my interest to wage war on Rome on his behalf.'

'Of course,' she said, 'you have your own agenda for extending your already enlarged kingdom.'

'That's right,' he affirmed.

'And may I ask how far you intend to extend it?'

'As far as to the south,' Tigranes said reluctantly.

'Thus you will obtain a mighty empire,' she said.

'There will be no more discussion on the subject, let this be the end of the matter!'

Just a few weeks later, Tigranes discovered from his agents that one of his sons, Zariadres, was trying to usurp the throne. He had built up a small force with the help of some of the nobility, who were unhappy with Tigranes' strong leadership. Just as the king had suspected, his hopes of durable peace within his kingdom were short-lived. 'How dare my own son think of revolting against his father?' he asked himself in amazement. Infuriated, he quickly sent his troops against the rebels, who were all killed. One of Tigranes' guards captured the rebel son and took him back to the city, where he was held in a prison.

The next day, the guard came back to him. 'Why did you want to betray your father?' he asked in a discourteous tone.

Zariadres remained silent, while the guard went on, 'Look, if you don't speak up, I will beat you to death.'

'It was my mother who has plotted the overthrow of my father,' the prince admitted.

'And you carried out the plot, but unsuccessfully, didn't you?'

After the son confessed his crime, he was executed for his treacherous deed.

Cleopatra had nurtured ambitions for Zariadres to succeed Tigranes, rather than the king's favourite son, Artavasdes II. So the queen conspired with nobles to topple her husband from the throne, because he had not given in to her pleas to help her father in his latest campaigns. Tigranes was informed of this conspiracy against his leadership but refrained from revealing it to his wife. From this point, it seemed to him that the nobility's influence was baneful, instead of being beneficial to his country. As a result of the rebellion, the king summoned to his palace some factions of the aristocracy, in an attempt to restore their loyalty to him and dispel hatred and division at home.

# CHAPTER 15

On another occasion, Tigranes went out hunting with two of his sons. He wore felt, non-metal headgear, depicting the coat of arms of Artaxiad. Cantering along the edges of the forest, the son named Tigranes the Young quickened his pace to a gallop, having seen a deer bounding some distance away.

Shortly afterwards, his father fell from his horse with a loud thud; the saddle was cinched loosely and had slipped. The impact of the fall caused him to lose consciousness, and his headgear to come free and drop to the ground. When he came round, Tigranes found his older son in a ridiculous posture; he had picked up the headgear and put it on his own head.

'Uh-oh! You wanted to take that from me, instead of rushing to my aid,' the father said, stunned by his son's disgraceful conduct.

'I was hoping to inherit the throne of Artaxiad one day, as your eldest son.'

Furious, Tigranes got up. 'I'm not obliged to choose you if I believe our gods desire otherwise.' He pulled his sword out of its sheath and struck his son dead. 'You foolish boy! I'm still the king,' he said.

It was his son's blind, pitiless indifference to his father's plight – and his preference for the headgear – which resulted in his death. The younger son, who had shot the deer with an arrow and returned to join his father, was shocked when he saw his brother lying dead on the ground.

'Oh no!' he stood motionless, stunned.

'I've killed him,' the father said, staring down at the corpse. 'So selfish was the boy that he didn't think of helping his father who had a nasty fall from his horse.'

'When did this all happen?'

'A while ago. After you left, my saddle suddenly slipped and I fell.'

'What was my brother doing then?'

'He'd picked up my headgear and put it on his head to show me he was the king. He deserved to die.'

The son expressed his profound regret at the unfortunate incident. When they returned to the palace, the king instructed his guard to collect the corpse and bury it secretly.

At this time, the Hasmonean Queen Salome Alexandra, last ruler of ancient Judea and known as the Iron Lady, had still territorial ambitions towards the previous Seleucid kingdom. As a result of Tigranes' incursions into the region, Alexandra conducted two unsuccessful military campaigns commanded by her younger son, Aristobulus II, against Ptolemy, the son of Mennaeus. Tigranes learned of her ambitions through his general, Magadates, who, by order of his leader, quickly neutralized the direct threat emanating from her actions and captured the city of

Damascus. After that, Tigranes turned his troops to the south and conquered Phoenicia. He used the southern port-city of Ptolemais as a base to prevent the Seleucids from coming to Salome Alexandra's aid, by cutting off land and sea access to Judea.

The Seleucid Queen Cleopatra Selene, once an ally to Queen Salome, who had ruled over Syria and instructed in vain the inhabitants to shut their gates against Tigranes, had escaped and taken refuge in Ptolemais – a region that had been under Selene's influence and sovereignty. With the capture of the city by Tigranes, she was arrested and immediately executed.

Judea was next in line, facing imminent invasion from Tigranes' armies. The news terrified Queen Salome, who had brought peace and prosperity to her nation during her nine years of reign. The Jewish leaders already envisaged Tigranes' fighters breaking through Jerusalem's walls and destroying the holy city, like the Neo-Babylonian King Nebuchadnezzar had done back in 586 BC. The recollection of their peoples' captivity in Babylon, where they had been held for decades and suffered greatly, intensified their panic. The queen paid tribute to Tigranes, sending him many valuable gifts, while Jewish envoys met him and entreated him to form good ties with their queen and nation, in the hope that he would refrain from attacking her kingdom. Tigranes made vague promises but he was actually reluctant to wage war against Judea, for he feared Salome's political alliances, especially with Rome.

# CHAPTER 16

After the entire territory of Pontus was effectively in Roman hands, and Lucullus' great victory celebration at Ephesus, he sent Appius Claudius – his arrogant, dissolute envoy and brother-in-law – to Antioch, in 70 BC. He was guided to the city from the upper mountains, along roundabout routes, by one of Tigranes' freemen. The envoy had been waiting a long time in Antioch for the emperor, to make a demand for Mithridates' extradition. He was also sent on a fact-finding mission, to gain a better understanding of the whole area for a possible invasion. Meanwhile, he secretly encouraged some of the head men of the neighbouring cities to shake off the yoke of Tigranes' tyranny and join the Romans in due course. He also won over a number of chiefs, who had unwillingly submitted to Tigranes.

When informed of Appius' arrival in Antioch, Tigranes was somewhat unwilling to hold a timely audience with the envoy. Nevertheless, clad in his comet-studded tiara, he rode his horse to his headquarters there, along with his four satrap-kinglets. As he sat on his throne, Appius was summoned to the sumptuous court of Achaemenid origin and abruptly handed over Lucullus' letter. Tigranes was troubled by this misbehaviour and the discourteous tone of the letter, in which he found out that Lucullus did not even address him as "King of Kings" or "Imperial Majesty" – a deliberate insult to him.

'Lucullus, general of the Roman army, has sent me to take charge of Mithridates and bring him to Rome as our prisoner,' Appius said bluntly.

'I know he's a cruel man but I must respect the alliance between us,' Tigranes replied with great moderation and continued, 'The King of Pontus has been my guest for more than a year, and he will stay in my domains as long as he wishes.'

'Surrender Mithridates now,' Appius demanded harshly.

Tigranes was taken aback by this freedom of speech. 'My own conscience would condemn me if I should surrender my father-in-law to the enemy,' he said with a forced smile.

'If you do not, Rome will declare war on you,' the envoy said haughtily.

The four kinglets, who stood around the throne with their arms folded across their chests, could sense their monarch's rage welling up inside him, and see how the envoy treated him with supercilious disdain.

'I know how to defend myself as always, but I wish for continued peace and friendship with Rome. I do not have any plans, never had, whatsoever, to expand westward,' Tigranes said calmly.

'Peace or war entirely depends on whether you hand over Mithridates or not.' Leaving no room for a proper negotiation, the emperor went on, 'You are dismissed now.'

The king sensed that Lucullus was trying to have him forced into a corner so that he could find an excuse for attacking his domains. Otherwise, he would have sent a more diplomatic envoy than Appius. However, an extended conflict with the Romans was the last thing the emperor desired.

The envoy, who only accepted a single bowl from among the splendid gifts offered by Tigranes, returned then to Pontus and delivered the king's letter to Lucullus. To get even with the latter, accordingly in his reply to him, he did not address him by the usual title of "Imperator". Enraged, the Roman commander felt compelled to carry out his ultimatum – pursue the fugitive war criminal and bring him to Rome. Simultaneously, he was preparing for an invasion of Tigranes' empire without Senatorial mandate to authorize such a move. Actually, he did not seek permission, for he knew such an invasion would have been seen in Rome as reckless and unnecessary. However, he would justify himself later to the Senate on the grounds that Tigranes, and not his subjects, was also his enemy, as the king refused to surrender his ally and would now have to pay the price for his behaviour. Moreover, he had been responsible for setting in motion the crisis in Cappadocia, by expelling Ariobarzanes.

It was actually Queen Salome, a shrewd politician, who aimed to keep Tigranes away from Judea. Fearing the invasion of her kingdom by his troops stationed in Phoenicia, she strongly encouraged Lucullus, her nominal ally at the time, to march against Tigranes. Apart from that, the Roman general was a greedy man, who wanted to slake his insatiable thirst for riches in the Near East. He was aware of the enormous wealth that awaited him in the many storehouses of Tigranes' palaces, and the treasures in the temples.

The final overthrow of Mithridates had opened the eyes

of Tigranes, and put him on his guard against the power of Rome. A possible invasion of his dominion by Lucullus prompted him to abruptly end his campaign in Phoenicia and return to Tigranocerta. The Pontic king, who had been held in captivity for a year and a half, was summoned to Tigranes' palace, where he had a private, lengthy discussion with him about the unpleasant audience he granted to Appius, and its political consequences. Mithridates tried to convince Tigranes that the Romans would not dare to come against him. Eventually, both kings thought that Lucullus' ultimatum was only a bluff and he could do nothing without the approval of the Senate, so they ignored the matter.

The conversation turned then to the mysterious death of Metrodorus of Scepsis, who had once been sent as an ambassador from Mithridates to Tigranes to seek help against the Romans. Metrodorus, famous for the power of his memory, was also a good friend of Tigranes, who had invited him to his court to write about his life. However, he refused to provide aid against his will, on the advice of the philosopher, who did not want the Pontic king to be saved, as a result of a bitter quarrel with him. As the man was killed on his way back to Pontus, the two allies strove to heal their mutual suspicions at the expense of other friends.

But in reality, Tigranes repented of what he had done, although he was not entirely to blame for the death of Metrodorus. He only gave an impulse to the hatred that his ally already had for the man. Nevertheless, Tigranes gave the body of the philosopher a grand burial, sparing no expense. After their informal meeting, which was held in a friendly mood, the Pontic king went back to his military camp to rebuild an army. Appius' arrogant behaviour and

Tigranes' rejection of his ally's surrender had immensely helped the cause of Mithridates in liberating all his domains from Roman occupation. With the generous aid of Tigranes' 7000 cavalrymen, he marched back into Pontus to recover the kingdom he had earlier lost.

# PART TWO
# The Fall

# CHAPTER 17

By this time, Tigranes had become the most powerful ruler of the Near East, after two-and-a-half decades of reign. His kingdom was now transformed into a vast empire, which was at the zenith of its power, stretching from the Caspian and Black Seas in the north to the Mediterranean Sea in the south, and from Great Media in the east to the mountainous Cilicia and part of Cappadocia in the west. Although his empire served as a buffer state between the Parthians and the Romans, its borders were both loosely controlled from Tigranocerta and sparsely defended by thousands of nomad warriors from innumerable warlike tribes; only a small portion of Tigranes' fighters were Armenians during this period.

The emperor was an admirer of great cities and he believed that the power of the state relied on the power of strong and prospering cities. He conducted a free trade policy within the Hellenistic cities, to which he granted autonomy, minting their own currency. But they were all judged according to the local laws and customs. Tigranes had brought many statues of deities back from his conquests. He was especially impressed by the aesthetic show and the grandeur of the Seleucid-Syrian civilization and religion. He must have thought there was some underlying similarity between the identities of Syrian deities and the Armenian ones. Thus, the king had enriched the national imperial pantheon, and enlarged it with such statues. These were added to the gilded copper Greek ones of Artemis and Apollo, which had once been brought by his grandfather, Artaxias I.

Tigranes introduced these images in his peoples' worship and no real fusion took place between the native and imported gods and goddesses. Those who obtained a wide popularity and had special places in the pantheon were the mother goddess Anahit, identified with the Greek Artemis, and Aramazd, corresponding with the Greek form of Zeus. In the temple, sacred fires were maintained, never extinguished, in front of which altars were set up to offer sacrifices and worship. The Jewish people did not agree, but if one of them were to dishonour the images, the emperor had the tongue of that person cut off.

Tigranes, who was residing at Tigranocerta, was incredulous at the unexpected news of the rapid advance of Lucullus' army from Asia Minor towards his domains. Unable to reconcile with this reality, he had the first person who brought the bad news beheaded, for being an alarmist and disturber of the good order of the cities. At this time, one of his trusted generals, Mithrobarzanes, informed his master that the Romans were really coming. Struck by his sincerity, Tigranes belatedly ordered him to slow down the enemy's advance and bring its commander to him alive. But Mithrobarzanes' forces of 3000 cavalrymen were crushed by Lucullus', both infantry and cavalry in equal proportion.

Having learned of Mithrobarzanes' defeat, Tigranes entrusted to Mancaeus the defence of his capital city and left for the Taurus Mountains to hastily recruit an army, but time was not on his side. Lucullus' legates disrupted two separate detachments, coming to the aid of the emperor, and engaged them in a canyon. The Roman commander, who handed command of Pontus to Sornatius, headed for Tigranocerta. He did not actually pursue Tigranes, for he had an unhindered path towards his capital, where he had left a regular guard (6000 heavy infantry) under Murena, to besiege the city. The Romans and their siege engines (siege breakers) that crept up to the fortress were occasionally driven off by naphtha thrown over them from the huge walls by the defenders.

A continuous shower of arrows poured upon the Roman army from the garrison and the setting of fire to the besieging machines put the Romans in a grave danger of Iranian warfare. Mancaeus, however, maintained the city, till Tigranes' army had assembled and come to break the siege. The Senate in Rome was more than astonished to hear that they were at war now with Tigranes the Great, and Lucullus had taken his army on a massive private plundering raid.

Tigranes marched with a large army back from Taurus towards his capital city. He had sent a few thousand of his horsemen ahead, who broke through Roman lines and rescued his concubines and the children he had by them – important political assets for the emperor. His general, Magadates, withdrew all troops from Cilicia and Syria to reinforce Tigranes' army in case of need. Meanwhile, Lucullus' army waded across the Euphrates – surprisingly at its lowest level – into the Tigranes-controlled principality of Sophene, without resistance. It was as though the population in that region were favourably disposed towards the Roman general traversing their territory. Lucullus pointed out to his soldiers Tigranes' stronghold in the distance and ordered them to destroy it. The two commanders, who made that journey of about 300 miles, were heading now to the same destination – the battlefield.

Tigranes first led his army towards a hill, the top of which was flat and broad, with gentle slopes reaching down to the plain. He stationed part of his infantry and cataphracts there and climbed with his two generals to the crest of the hill, overlooking Tigranocerta. As he observed the view of his capital, its forcibly transplanted inhabitants, who saw the Romans as liberators, stood on the walls of the fortress, greeting Tigranes with shouts. They were alerting the approaching Romans to the location of his army.

# CHAPTER 18

In 69 BC, on October 6$^{th}$ at daybreak, the weather was clear when the two armies of Tigranes and Lucullus lined up on opposite sides of the Batman River, south-west of the capital city Tigranocerta. Tigranes' Imperial Army (210,000 soldiers), half of which consisted of Iberians, the other half of Albanians and Medes, was positioned on the east bank of the river. The army was formed of three sections: two of his vassal kings of Adiabene and Medes led the left and right flanks, at the rear of which were positioned Tigranes' 50,000 cavalrymen or cataphracts. The 140,000-strong heavy infantry – forcibly recruited peasants from various regions – formed a second line of his army. The third line consisted of 20,000 mounted archers and slingers. Behind them were the camp followers – army service providers.

Lucullus' army (30,000 men), half of which consisted of Thracian and Galatian irregulars, and Bithynian horsemen, the other half of Roman and skilled Fimbrian legions, was deployed on the west bank of the river in a single line. The Romans were dressed in red, their silver helmets derived from Gallic designs. Tigranes was surprised by Lucullus' amazing temerity to meet his multitudinous forces, which exceeded seven times those of the Roman legions altogether.

Mithridates, astonished to hear about Lucullus' invasion of Tigranes' dominion from his agents, urgently sent his most trusted general, Taxiles, to his ally's headquarters. After learning he was with his army at the riverbank, he hurried to join him there.

'Mithridates urges you to stay on the defensive, harass the enemy's forces and cut off their provisions,' the general said with meaning. 'You could surround and starve the Roman army by means of your cavalry.'

Tigranes hearkened to his advice with patience. He then gestured to Taxiles at the diminutive Roman force and said with a contemptuous laugh, 'If that's a diplomatic mission, it's too big. If it's an army, it's too small for me.'

'Beware of those Roman legions! They're highly disciplined and veteran soldiers.' The general warned Tigranes not to be over-confident of victory over the Romans.

Lucullus, an astute tactician, knew that Tigranes' heavily armoured cataphracts posed the greatest threat to his men, and they had to be neutralized. Using a clever military strategy prior to combat engagement, he left one of his legates in command of his forces near the river and ordered him to conduct a feint retreat from there.

Tigranes mistakenly believed that the Romans were leaving the battlefield. He turned to Taxiles and said, unsurprised, 'Looks like they're backing off now.'

The general shook his head, 'Definitely not,' he said. 'The movement of the Romans in maniples is only an indication of immediate action. Besides, they are in full battle dress, not in their marching gear.'

The emperor seemed to be off-balance. 'You really think so?' he asked, trying to play down the seriousness of the situation on the ground.

'I wish Your Majesty good fortune, and may this day work a miracle in your favour,' Taxiles said and left.

Tigranes wondered why Lucullus had vanished from sight. He checked his troops in preparation for making a possible headlong charge at the Romans, thinking he had the advantage in the open fight.

Meanwhile, the Roman general knew there was no time to lose and that he should act immediately. Armed with a steel cuirass and his coat of arms on the shield, with two cohorts he crossed, unnoticed, the shallowest part of the stream, which lay higher up, where it curved westward and was easily fordable. Thus, he gained the high ground – the eastern bank of Tigranes' right flank. The Roman forces raced at top speed across the plain and outflanked the rest of Tigranes' cavalry, stationed on the slopes of a hill. Circled by reverse (anticlockwise), the cavalrymen were taken by surprise and were unable to reposition quickly enough to face the enemy.

The unexpected attack by the Romans from the rear became the critical decisive factor and tipped the balance of the war in their favour. Lucullus, upon reaching the top of the hill, drew his shining sword and shouted across to his soldiers so as to buoy their morale, 'The day is ours, my fellow soldiers! I assure you, we're victorious.' A Roman legion then used the tuba (Roman trumpet) and Lucullus bellowed out the order to his troops to beat down the enemy's lances with their swords and attack the legs and thighs of its cataphracts – the only areas of the horses which were unarmoured. The Roman general quickly charged downwards, and Tigranes' cataphracts were attacked. Some of them fell off and, weighed down by heavy armour, could not get back up. The other lumbering cataphracts, in their attempt to break free from the attackers, fell with their unwieldy horses upon the ranks of their infantry.

A few moments later, the sound of galloping horses could be heard from the rear of Tigranes' army stationed on the riverbank. All his soldiers looked back and saw Lucullus' cohorts coming at full speed towards them. 'Are they on us?' the bewildered emperor exclaimed in disbelief.

Panic spread throughout the line of his army, which began to collapse, as his vassal kings and nobles deserted him in haste for Roman protection. As a result of calculated attacks by the Romans, Tigranes' army disintegrated in a matter of hours, and he himself took to flight northwards.

Meanwhile, Mancaeus, the commander of the garrison of Tigranocerta, who was informed of the dispersal of Tigranes' army, had serious doubts about the loyalty of his Greek mercenaries to protect the city. In fact, the exasperated and disgruntled guards suddenly opened the gates of Tigranocerta to the invading enemy. Lucullus' army began the wholesale looting and destruction of the city's cultural wealth – proof that the Romans cared little about the Hellenistic high ideals. The royal treasury, estimated to be worth 8000 talents in gold, was reserved for Lucullus, but Tigranes had already managed to spirit part of it away. Each Roman soldier was awarded by his commander 800 drachmas from the spoils, after which the city was set ablaze. The abundant quantity of gold and silver from the melted-down statues, pots and the like was then carried off to Rome as war booty.

The Roman general had protected many of the wives of Tigranes' chief officers, keeping them safe from harm and thus winning their husbands to his side. He allowed the Greeks, Cappadocians and others, forcibly transported to the city, to return home. On the other hand, the many players Tigranes had brought to the theatre, Lucullus used for his interludes and triumphs. The casualties and losses for the battle of Tigranocerta were disproportionate, with no exact numbers. According to reliable sources, it was estimated that there were between 10,000 and 50,000 deaths on Tigranes' side. His forces, which far exceeded Lucullus', were heavily defeated by the Roman legions – a classical example of quality triumphing over quantity.

# CHAPTER 19

The battle and fall of Tigranocerta had resulted in significant territorial losses of Tigranes' vast empire. Most of his imperial dominions to the south of the Taurus Mountains, together with his eastern conquests, fell under the sway of Rome and reduced to the status of Roman provinces. Actually, the reason for this unauthorized invasion was to achieve Lucullus' multiple aims: to put an end to the so-called barbarian hordes, on the pretext of bringing civilization to the Near East, hunt for fortune and glory, and punish Tigranes for challenging Rome's power, as well as harbouring its great enemy, Mithridates. Despite the huge losses Tigranes suffered, the battle did not end the war.

Halfway to the Tigris valley, Mithridates, who was belatedly coming to the aid of Tigranes with 10,000 cavalrymen, met a trickle of his ally's panicked troops, making off in the opposite direction of the battlefield. They informed him of their king's humiliating defeat. Anxious only for his safety, he had fled from the battleground. Mithridates went in search of his friend and found him alone further along the road. In dread of falling into the hands of his enemy, Tigranes had stripped off his royal tiara, which one of his faithful servants took to Artaxata.

Mithridates cantered towards him and jumped from his horse. As Tigranes' distraught features gazed at him, they quickly hugged each other. When they released their hold, Tigranes saw at a distance some of his wounded soldiers, fleeing northwards. With tears welling up in his eyes, he turned to Mithridates and said solemnly, 'I've lost everything... my city, Tigranocerta, my army, just everything.'

'I'm so sorry,' Mithridates said, putting his hand on Tigranes' shoulder. Eager to learn about the exact cause of his defeat, he asked, 'What did happen? Have you engaged yourself in open fight with the Romans?'

Tigranes shook his head, 'There was no real fight, but a flight.'

'What do you mean?'

'The unexpected attack on my army changed the whole situation on the ground.'

'I don't understand.'

'Apparently, Lucullus' men had crossed the river unnoticed and thus gained our right flank. They were upon us then from the rear. I tried to adjust my battle line but it was too late,' Tigranes said.

'Damn! Clever military strategy, isn't it? I know about those Roman legions better than you do; I've learned something from my failures, too, in my long, bloody wars with them.'

The Pontic king ordered his personal guard to bring a horse to his friend, with clear instructions to look after his downhearted relative. While the two defeated kings were riding towards Artaxata, Mithridates refrained from criticizing Tigranes in his misfortunes. In need of the goodwill of his son-in-law more than ever, he consoled and encouraged him. 'Don't worry, we'll assemble another big army and fight them back in guerrilla warfare this time.'

'That's the only way now to secure a victory over the Romans,' Tigranes replied.

The two war fugitives, still energetic and ambitious, devoted themselves to raising a new army. Tigranes was determined to continue the war and entrusted his ally with its political and military management. Having recruited many warriors from Armenia and warlike tribes of Colchis and Caucasus, the two kings summoned these Asiatic recruits and urged them to protect the east and its gods from the impious Roman invaders. While they were trained as cavalrymen and infantrymen, the remaining local people were set to produce bows and poisonous arrows for their archers. Tigranes and Mithridates agreed to use the Parthian battle tactics and fight against the Romans independently but in coordination with each other. The two allies were determined to revenge their defeat by delivering a major blow to Lucullus.

They separately sent envoys to the Parthian king, Phraates III, and proposed an alliance with him, soliciting money, more troops and weapons, of which Parthia had great resources. The message was that if they were defeated, Parthia would never be able to resist Rome, and it was in the king's best interests to help them. Lucullus, who had heard about the sending of envoys by his two foe kings, also dispatched his own envoy to Phraates and urged him to remain neutral. In fact, they had already reached an agreement that the Euphrates was the boundary between Rome and Parthia. Ultimately, the Parthian king ended up giving no support to Tigranes and Mithridates, for many internal and external reasons. For one, he felt resentment against Tigranes for having once invaded northern Mesopotamia and stripping the Parthians' previous monarch of his title King of Kings.

In the following week, Mithridates sent a letter to Phraates, in which he incited him against the Romans. 'The Romans have waged wars everywhere, they devastated people's homes, robbed their temples and brought a faction of the lower-class population to Rome as slaves. They either beguiled or thwarted the schemes of their enemies to impose direct Roman rule in their cities.

'The Romans are uncivilized barbarians and have no culture. If together, you, in Mesopotamia, and we, in Armenia, besiege their armies, cut off the provisions of those Romans, who have been saved so far only by their victories and our own errors, you would then have the reputation of boldly having assisted two great kings and suppressed a greedy invader. So I implore you to ally with us, unless you would rather by our ruin further expand the Roman Empire than by our friendship become a national hero yourself.'

Unfortunately, the letter remained unanswered.

# CHAPTER 20

About a year later, in September 68 BC, Lucullus moved his troops northward to attack the important city of Artaxata, where Tigranes' present headquarters were located. In the hope of compelling the king to fight either on the way or at any rate before Artaxata, he threatened through a messenger his hereditary residence – wives, children domiciled there and the treasures of his court. When Tigranes showed himself neither ready to make peace, nor surrender, Lucullus marched deeper into Armenia's unfamiliar highlands. Leading his troops along the eastern shore of Lake Van, into the valley of the eastern Euphrates, he reached the Murat River (the ancient name being Arsanias). The Roman general, a pious man, made sacrifices to the gods before he marched out of his camp for a pitched battle. Tigranes' and Mithridates' joint forces – the mounted archers and Iberian lance-men led by the former himself and the light cavalry led by the latter – advanced towards the opposite bank of the river.

At this point, Lucullus was taken by surprise when he faced the enemy's new contingent of forces. As he crossed the river, he was first confronted by Tigranes' mounted archers who, in a feigned retreat, suddenly twisted backwards on their horses and shot at the Romans. In an initial skirmish, the Roman legions endeavoured to strike at the flanks of the archers. Then the two fugitive allies continually harassed their common enemy with hit-and-run actions, refraining from attacking them head-on. After several short skirmishes, they pulled back their forces into the hillside, luring the enemy to pursue them in vain.

The Roman army received irreparable damage and the general was forced to withdraw his troops to the south in November. He then laid siege to Nisibis, another treasure city of Tigranes', whose brother Guras had been directing the defence. Upon the news of Lucullus' retreat, the irrepressible Mithridates took this opportunity to re-occupy Pontus and realize his long-awaited dream of empire-building around the Black Sea. He marched his army of 6000 men towards Zela, where the Romans had not expected him to strike at them, as the revengeful king caught several small Roman detachments there. The Roman legate, Fabius, endeavoured to defeat Mithridates in battle, but his garrison army suffered a counterblow by the Pontic forces. The Romans having lost hundreds of their men, Fabius sent out desperate messengers to his general, Lucullus, and to the legate Triarius. The latter arrived in Pontus and took command of all Roman forces there.

At Zela, near which the battle took place on a plain, the joint-army of Triarius and Fabius marched on Mithridates' camp. The Pontic king fought first against one section of the advancing enemy and, after defeating them, led his cavalry round the rear of the remaining forces and broke them too. The Pontic troops then drove the Romans back into a trench that Mithridates' men had dug in advance, filling it back with earth. Trapped in a cycle of unprecedented violence, thousands of Roman soldiers were killed in what became a long and brutal fight, and another trench was soon clogged up with their corpses. While Mithridates suffered a near-fatal wound, the rest of the Romans fled, having endured heavy defeats.

The locals, having experienced the merciless yoke of the enemy, welcomed the return of their Pontic king with joy. The latter then fell back to the fortress of Talaura in Armenia Minor and awaited reinforcements by Tigranes. Once he received the extra troops of his ally, he marched back to Pontus to liberate his kingdom from pockets of resistance to his forces. As Rome was aware of the provision of army by Tigranes to Mithridates, ill feelings towards the former increased and aggravated the situation in Asia Minor.

The summer was unusually short, as the first snows fell in autumn and temperatures dropped significantly. The Romans were unaccustomed to the exceptionally harsh Armenian winter. When Lucullus learned about his defeat in Pontus, he broke camp to fight back against Mithridates. With little profit and insufficient food supply, the general's troops under Publius Clodius mutinied and refused to advance any further. They complained about years of impulsive campaigns and marches of 950 miles, and told their leader to continue the war on his own. Moreover, the accusations which sprang up against the general in Rome, found a dangerous echo in his legionnaires' quarters. They were exasperated by rumours circulating that their leader was also planning an expedition against the Parthians. In fact, Lucullus not only failed to bring the Pontic king to Rome as a trophy but also had misjudged the time needed for a campaign encroaching so far into the Armenian highlands. Frustrated by the decreasing morale of his troops, he gave up his pursuit of Mithridates, thus being unable to come to the rescue of his two legate-governors trapped in Pontus.

King Mithridates I of Media Atropatene, a third son of Tigranes and Cleopatra, who married his sister – a princess from the Artaxiad dynasty – supported his father by joining forces with the Pontic king to invade Cappadocia for the third time. After facing resistance by the Romans, the joint armies succeeded in annexing only the northern parts of that territory.

Since the helpless Lucullus could not cope with the situation in Asia Minor, he was recalled to Rome a year later. Having accumulated an enormous treasure from his Eastern campaigns, which were seen as massive, private plundering raids, he lavishly spent money on personal villas in Naples and arranged great feasts for his friends and political opponents. The general was accused by the Roman Senate of using state money illegally and making one war out of another in vain, so as to longer retain the command in his hands. According to the Senate, he should have pursued Tigranes and Mithridates immediately after the victory in Tigranocerta – without giving them time to raise new troops – and driven them out of their domains, bringing this particular war to an end. The province of Cilicia was taken from Lucullus and assigned to proconsul Quintus Marcius Rex.

The proconsul, pressured by his brother-in-law, Publius

Clodius – a Roman politician of the late Republic – categorically refused to help Lucullus. Marcius took three new legions to his province and eventually achieved nothing. During this time the pirates had grown so much stronger that they controlled many cities around the shores.

# CHAPTER 21

In 66 BC, Marcus Tullius Cicero - the Roman praetor/statesman, orator and philosopher - made an important speech to support Pompey as a competent leader and talented strategist, having a great knowledge of warfare. The purpose of the speech was to encourage people to vote for the lex Manilia. In his oratory, Cicero pointed to the necessity and difficulty of the war against Mithridates, which he believed Pompey was best equipped to conduct.

'I'm now one of the praetors of this year. My previous speeches had all been legal cases, and this is my first-ever contio speech. Let's start with the cause of Mithridates and the war in Asia Minor. Two triumphs for Sulla and Murena have come out of this, but both were recalled to Rome: Sulla by a crisis at home, and Murena by Sulla. As for Mithridates, he remained on his throne and used his grace period to re-arm. Lucullus then defeated Mithridates at Cyzicus and sank his massive fleet, thus opening the way for our legions into Pontus, where they captured Sinope and many other cities. This forced the Pontic king to take refuge in Tigranes' Armenia. Later, the pugnacious Mithridates marched back into Pontus and attacked our army again. Can you imagine that? We're not going to let pass the genocidal slaughter of tens of thousands of our citizens in Asia Minor by Mithridates and the horribly torturous death of Manius Aquillius.

'The public are extremely worried, and we badly need a new general. Guess who he is! Like our ancestors, we have to defend our allies: Ariobarzanes, for example, who's been driven into exile many times – first by Tigranes and then by Mithridates. If we don't get Asia back, think of the dire financial situation we will find ourselves in. We have to protect the interests of our citizens, whose property is affected by war, and recover our popularity abroad, which has been seriously affected by the bad behaviour of our governors. Pompey stands head and shoulders above the rest and possesses all the qualities of a perfect general, who has done battle everywhere, in every sea, and bested all his enemies. I believe he's a great strategist and has the best leadership skills, so why would you hesitate to give him full command of the war?'

The lex Manilia law, proposed in the same year by the tribune Gaius Manilius, eventually passed, transferring the exclusive authority for the Eastern campaign to Pompey.

Since then, Lucullus and Pompey had become greater enemies than ever. A conversation between them, which had started with mutual marks of politeness and amity, had gradually turned into an angry exchange of insults. Lucullus made bitter complaints of the newly appointed general, who severely reproached him for being avaricious and doing anything to satisfy his never-ending thirst for wealth. For both of them, however, there was nothing greater than winning honour, glory and fame.

Pompey took over and arrived in the various sections of the Mediterranean with a large contingent of ships. In a difficult but brilliant three-month operation, as given by the Senate to complete his mission, he annihilated the entire pirate fleet and bases at the shores of Cilicia. His success brought him an even more important command. He was to defeat the two foe invader kings – Mithridates and Tigranes – in Asia Minor, which was in a state of unrest and anarchy. The general sent his envoy to the former and demanded his surrender, and the handing over of the Roman deserters. The Pontic king requested a truce in the hope that he could win to his side the new Parthian king, Phraates III. To his great disappointment, he learned that the king had already entered into friendship with Pompey, who had been trying to convince him in vain to invade Armenia in order to turn Tigranes' attention to protecting his own kingdom and leave the issue of Mithridates to him.

Since the harsh terms proposed by Pompey were unacceptable to Mithridates, the Roman leader wanted him to suffer an overwhelming defeat, for he had been an embarrassing mess so far. He sent three legions to secure first Cappadocia and then marched his numerically superior army towards Pontus, where the king's selected troops of 30,000 foot soldiers and 3000 cavalrymen were stationed on his frontier. Once more, the tuba was used to convey information on the march, in the field and in camp.

Pompey placed a cavalry force in ambush at the border and harassed the enemy's outposts openly. The king, being short of provisions, retreated reluctantly, allowing Pompey to enter his territory. He expected him to suffer from scarcity when encamped in the devastated region, but the Roman commander had already arranged to have his supplies sent after him. After establishing a number of fortified posts and camps, he approached Mithridates' camp, where an engagement broke out between them in a narrow valley. Some of the Pontic cavalrymen fought the Romans dismounted until a contingent of Roman-allied cavalry arrived.

Fearing that the Pontic king would seek shelter in Armenia with his ally, Tigranes, the Roman commander launched a clever, unexpected night attack, in which many Pontic soldiers were killed in the fighting. Eventually, at Dasteria (Nicopolis), Pompey heavily defeated Mithridates, who amazingly escaped by night into the thick woods, along with a few thousand cavalrymen. Given that his forces now were much inferior, he continued withdrawing, and entered Lesser Armenia. Pompey followed him and set up a successful ambush there after he was joined by more Roman forces.

The Pontic king then fled in disarray to the coast of northern Colchis, instead of taking refuge in Armenia, because Tigranes categorically refused this time to offer shelter to him, despite Cleopatra's further pleas for her father's life.

Since Mithridates' overwhelming loss in Pontus, which marked almost his final collapse, relations between him and his ally had strained to breaking point. Tigranes felt that his father-in-law had become increasingly burdensome to him and even offered a reward for his capture, for he feared Roman retribution. As was common in the Ancient Near East, family ties resulting from royal marriages between ruling kings or dynasties did not necessarily assure political alliances and alignments, with the threat of enemy aggression.

It was during this period that Tigranes' fourth son – Tigranes the Young – raised a rebellion against his father. Hoping to receive the crown of Armenia, he went to join the Parthians and desperately persuaded King Phraates III, whose daughter he had married, to invade Armenia in an attempt to place him on the throne. However, Artaxata was well defended when the prince led a Parthian army to besiege the capital. They soon retreated as they realized the city would not fall without a long siege, the time for which their king could not spare as he feared plots at home. King Tigranes, who had withdrawn into the hills, hurried back and drove his son out of his domain. The rebel prince, after learning that the Pontic king, his maternal grandfather, had also been defeated and was unable to help him, fled to Pompey. The latter, who had lost track of Mithridates, presumed dead, under pretence of supporting the prince, joined him to guide his 50,000-strong army into Armenia.

# CHAPTER 22

In 65 BC, the Roman army under Pompey stood at the walls of Artaxata without bloodshed. King Tigranes was quickly informed by his agents that his eponymous son had accompanied Pompey's army. He was deeply disappointed by his son's treacherous act, not to mention the earlier betrayal by his two eldest sons. Several noblemen from the Artaxiad dynasty, who feared for their lives, joined the Roman camp. Now in his mid-seventies, the king did not have the will, nor did he hold the winning cards, to fight another war. He knew that his personal glory was to be secondary when it came to the long-term interests of his kingdom and people. Although capitulation was difficult for him to accept, he had no choice but to sign a peace treaty with Pompey, to spare the city of Artaxata from suffering the same fate as Tigranocerta. He learned about the general's leniency, and that he was fair and reasonable in his negotiations. He gathered what was left of the members of his court and explained to them his reasons for submitting to Rome.

The king then sent a delegation to Pompey to pave the

way for a meeting with him. The Roman general warmly received the delegates and said he would be happy to talk to their king. Tigranes discarded his purple mantle and wore only his royal tiara. Together with a Roman escort, he rode on his white horse to Pompey's military camp, which was sixteen miles away from Artaxata. At the entry to the camp, two lictors came out, one of them saying firmly, 'No living man has ever entered a Roman camp on horseback.'

The other lictor ordered him to dismount: 'Get down from your horse and surrender your sword.'

The king obeyed and, unbuckling his sword, he handed it over to the lictor. He then proceeded on foot towards Pompey's tent, near which one of his guards stood, expressionless. When Tigranes entered the tent, the Roman general was seated in splendorous fashion, while the treacherous son had taken a seat to the left of him. Two of the general's high-ranking officers were standing just behind them. Upon seeing his father, the prince did not even stand up. The king approached and bowed to Pompey, who was impressed by his courage.

'There's no man in Rome or any other country that I'd have surrendered to, except the victorious Pompey,' Tigranes said. 'I'd be content with any fortune, whether it is good or bad.'

He then took off his royal tiara and laid it near his feet. He was about to cast himself down to prostrate before the general in supplication when Pompey, touched by compassion, leaped up. 'Please don't do that,' he said, holding the king by the hand. 'Rise,' he added, lifted him up in admiration, and gently put the tiara back on Tigranes' head. The son watched enviously while Pompey gestured for his father to sit to his right side and proclaimed magnanimously, 'I, Pompey the Great, acknowledge you as King of Greater Armenia on condition that you renounce your claims on all your conquests, except for Sophene, Gordyene and the seventy valleys.'

'I have no disparaging comments about my heavy losses,' Tigranes said, his eyes downcast.

'If your territory has been much reduced, you must blame that on Lucullus.'

'Anyway, I do not think it is dishonourable to surrender to you. I guess the gods of providence are on your side now,' Tigranes said.

'I'm afraid so, but I allow you to retain your kingdom and hold what you've kept up to the present time, if you pay six thousand talents to the Romans as a penalty for the expenses of war.'

Tigranes reflected on the hard terms imposed on him, while Pompey went on, 'You will be recognized as a friend and ally of the Roman people.'

Pompey turned to the son, 'As for you, you will be the king of Sophene, but its treasure will go to your father so he will be able to pay his fine.'

Lowering his head with anger, the son was discontented, for he had expected Pompey to give him the throne of Greater Armenia. Finally, a peace treaty was signed between Tigranes and Pompey.

The Roman general, having disposed of the Kingdom of Armenia, put the rebel prince in chains for having rudely refused his order to be the King of Sophene. He then launched his Iberian campaign and marched his army northward towards its strongholds. The Artaxiad king Artoces of Iberia, who had once gone to war with Rome on the side of the Pontic king and Tigranes, was alarmed by the invasion of the Romans and the seizing of the fortress of Harmozike. The Iberian king tried to turn to diplomacy and promised Pompey unconditional friendship, but the latter was alerted by his agents that the Iberians were secretly planning an attack on him. The Roman general then marched his forces into the centre of Iberia, where the battle took place near the Pelorus River.

The Romans first met a stout and vigorous resistance from the king's troops, which suffered heavy casualties. Artoces, realizing the situation was getting out of hand, managed to escape and asked for a truce. Pompey demanded the king's children as hostages, threatening him to inflict more damage on his army if he refused to comply with his demand. Eventually, the king submitted and, giving up his children, he signed a peace treaty with the Romans under which the Kingdom of Iberia, like the Kingdom of Armenia, was to be a friend and ally of the Roman Republic.

After Pompey conquered the kingdoms of Colchis and Albania, he marched his troops back westward to resume the hunt for Mithridates. Having wintered on the border between Iberia and Colchis, the general realized the great difficulties of the voyage with no means of subsistence to his troops by land or sea, and gave up his further pursuit of the fugitive king.

Returning by the coast to Pontus, he found lots of treasures there, which had been abandoned by the flight of Mithridates. After Bithynia, Pontus, Colchis, Iberia and Albania became Roman protectorates, Pompey's legates and officers entered Syria and beyond in 65/64 BC to assert Roman control over Tigranes' former possessions. Later in that year, the general himself marched into the region, which paved the way for a new epoch in the history of Rome's Eastern expansion. The Roman general had categorically rejected the Parthian king's request to recognize the Euphrates as the limit of Roman control. In violation of his treaty with him, he annexed a part of the Parthian territory between the Euphrates and the Tigris River.

In fact, Mithridates' warning letter to his Parthian counterpart, Phraates III, back in 69 BC, turned out to be an amazing reality.

# CHAPTER 23

Tigranes learned that his long-time ally, Mithridates, was still alive. In fact, the defeated Pontic king, knowing that the King of Armenia had abandoned him, and in consequence of his submission to Pompey, had spent the whole winter in Colchis at the stronghold of Dioscurias. In the following spring, he made his way through all the northern coastal tribes of the Black Sea and reached Panticapaeum (modern-day Kerch), the capital of his own kingdom of Bosporus in the Crimea. One of his sons, Machares, who ruled the kingdom as viceroy and feared that his father would punish him for having offered earlier assistance to Lucullus in the siege of Sinope, committed suicide.

Mithridates, to his generals' amazement, was still planning an overland invasion of Rome with an army of Scythians, by the Danube and the Alps. To accomplish his military project, he met princes in the coastal dynastic cities and made alliances with them through his young daughters' engagements to the heirs. But not long after, he gave up his project when he learned about the treachery of his second younger son, Pharnaces II, who also colluded with the Romans to seize the throne.

Alone in a citadel with his two engaged daughters, Nysa and Mithridates, born from their father's concubines, the hopeless king uncapped the hollow compartment in the hilt of his sword and tipped out a little golden vial.

'What's that?' Nysa asked.

'Poison, I want to end my life,' he said in despair as he opened the bottle.

The two young girls, who had been betrothed to the kings of Ptolemaic Egypt and of Cyprus, taken aback and unhappy with their own lives too, insisted together, 'We would like to have some of it first.'

Amazed at their insistence, the father handed them the vial. As they sipped a few doses in turn, the drug took effect on them at once. After watching them die, the king swallowed the rest. But the attempt failed for him because of his long life of self-administered antidotes, which strengthened his immunity to poison. He said to himself, 'I, the absolute monarch of so great a kingdom, am now unable to poison myself because I foolishly used other drugs as antidotes.'

He took his sword to stab himself to death but was unsuccessful due to his physical weakness and psychological distress. He then called one of his Gaulish bodyguards, Bituitus, and said, 'I have profited much from your strong right arm, which kept me safe from my enemies in the past. I shall profit from the same arm if you will kill me now and spare me the humiliation of being led in a Roman triumph.'

His bodyguard looked at him and hesitated for a moment.

'Please render me the service I so much desire, and have

no regrets,' Mithridates said firmly.

Bituitus, deeply moved, drew then his sword and thrust it forcefully into Mithridates' belly. As blood gushed from the fatal wound, the king said his last words, 'Thank you,' and collapsed to the ground.

Learning about Mithridates' death, Pompey journeyed hastily to the east coast of Pontus from Palestine. He surprisingly took a decision there to provide funds for a proper funeral for his foe, whose body was transferred by Pharnaces from Panticapaeum to Sinope in 63 BC, along with his royal trappings – armour, helmet, purple cloak, ornate sword and sceptre. Pompey was astonished at the magnificence of the armours and raiment that the Pontic king used to wear. The general refused to inspect the corpse, which, after the passage of some months, was decomposed and unrecognizable except for the scar from the sword gash on his belly and the royal insignia. The sending of the body was the price of Pompey's recognition of Pharnaces' claim to Pontus.

Mithridates was buried in the royal sepulchre of his forefathers, thus ending the reign of one of Rome's most enduring and elusive enemies. The dauntless old king's inhuman feats and acts of heroism, combined with gruesome deeds of murder, had also ended with him. He was long remembered as a legend in his own time, a symbol of uncompromising defiance, and an unfortunate victim of Roman imperialism. In 63 BC, after the death of Mithridates, Pompey was free to plan the consolidation of the Eastern provinces and kingdom borders. Taking into account the geographical and political factors involved in the region, he imposed an overall settlement to last, with a few changes, for more than 525 years.

Two years later, in 61 BC, Pompey was treating the obnoxious Tigranes the Young coldly. Despite the intercession of King Phraates III – the prince's father-in-law – the Roman commander took him to Rome as a prisoner, for the offence given to him, and his accomplices' refusal to grant his father and the Romans access to the royal treasures in Sophene. In a spectacular parade, which marked Pompey's third and final triumph, leaders of the pirates, noblemen, sons of the kings, who had been taken as hostages – 400 in all – walked in their native costumes ahead of Pompey, who sat on a lofty gem-studded chariot. Among them were Tigranes the Young with his wife and daughter, a wife and sister of Tigranes the Great, and five children of Mithridates VI, captured in the Bosporan kingdom.

Following Pompey's chariot were his officers on horseback. Behind them, hundreds of carts rolled, many carrying arms and beaks of warships. Others were loaded high with gold and great treasures, like the golden statues of Mars and Apollo, all plundered from the cities of the East. The quantity of gold bullion, dragged along in the procession, was greater than any general had brought to Rome before. It was sufficient to provide generous bounties for all his soldiers, leaving much for the treasury.

Of those who were absent from the parade; King Mithridates and King Tigranes, among others, large images of them with the Eupator's royal trappings were carried aloft in the procession, representing them as fugitive vanquished fighters – a degrading public display. For the local Italians, who enjoyed the parade in huge numbers, the Roman commander seemed to boast of his great Eastern military victories. He had accomplished what his predecessors had failed to do – bringing about the death of Mithridates and the surrender of Tigranes.

After the parade, all captives were sent back to their homes, except the kings. One of them, Aristobulus II, the Jewish king from the Hasmonean dynasty, was put to death, and later Tigranes the Young suffered the same fate. The culmination of this historical procession was a sacrifice of a number of white bulls to the chief god of the Roman state, Jupiter, at his temple on the Capitoline Hill in the centre of the city. In making this ultimate sacrifice, Pompey thanked the god for his support of Rome and its military success.

# CHAPTER 24

King Tigranes himself was restricted to his hereditary kingdom after the many battles he had fought until his mid-seventies. He had paid the penalty money he owed the Romans; 10,000 drachmas to each military tribune, 1000 drachmas for each centurion, and fifty for each legionary. He received then several tokens of the victor's appreciation and respect.

Seated upon the throne, all alone in his palace, and faced with the reality of the situation, the king looked back on the important turning points in his life. He cast his mind back to his coronation ceremony in a vision, then pictured the scene in which he addressed his troops, constructing some of his speech, 'Everyone in this army is important and plays a vital role. We shall defend to the death our native land and fight together with confidence and strength. We shall not admit defeat nor contemplate surrender.'

At this point, he re-experienced the major past events through successive mental images. Starting with his conquests of Armenia's neighbouring kingdoms, and the indirect involvement of his forces in Roman provinces on behalf of his ally, he recalled some of the argument Cleopatra had with him in their royal bedchamber.

'I think you didn't adequately back my father on his three wars with the Romans. The last one proved to be a humiliating defeat for him,' she said.

'I couldn't commit myself at this stage to supplying him with extra troops,' Tigranes replied.

'Why not?'

'Because my forces, as you probably know, are already stretched too thin throughout my domains. They also need to safeguard the southern border with Parthia on one hand and against the attacks by the northern tribes on the other.'

'You forged an alliance with my father,' Cleopatra reminded her husband, 'and a treaty of mutual defence and support was signed after our marriage, remember?'

'Yes, but I've already carried out my part of the bargain, and it's not in my interest to wage war on Rome on his behalf.'

The last words echoed in Tigranes' mind, after which he moved on to the unpleasant audience he held with Lucullus' envoy, Appius Claudius, and then to the battle of Tigranocerta.

He recalled the envoy's harsh demand: 'Surrender Mithridates now. If you do not, Rome will declare war on you.' The warning rang twice in his mind. He wondered if his alliance with Mithridates had been a political blunder in the first place, and if he had made another mistake by rejecting his extradition. But he thought even if he had acceded to Appius' demand, the Roman general would have pursued his political ambition to dominate the Near East for Roman supremacy in the region. That's exactly what happened; what Lucullus had started, Pompey finished off. Lust for glory and domination, the Romans did not hesitate to die for their sake.

Tigranes knew that the recruited men in his new army, apart from his cavalry, had not enough combat experience to confront the enemy at the battle of Tigranocerta. Although he greatly relied on his multitudinous forces, a reckless, headlong charge at the enemy was not always a good option for him, unless he was sure that such a military action would be successful. In fact, the unexpected attack by the Romans from the rear became the one critical decisive key factor in the disintegration of his army and marked the beginning of his downfall. For a moment, he was thinking how he rose to heights of imperial glory with audacity and determination, then lived his last years as an adjunct of the foes who, externally or at home, cut him down to size.

Tigranes retained the title of King of Kings, which, after all, he gave to himself, and continued to rule another ten years over his original dominion, as an ally and a friend of the Roman Empire. Although he engaged in frontier disputes with Parthia, he remained a peaceful vassal of Rome until his own death in 55 BC.

Pompey had fully assigned Gordyene to Armenia Major back in 63/62 BC and conferred the territory of Armenia Minor upon Deiotarus, the king of Galatia, who was a friend of Rome in the Third Mithridatic War. Moreover, the general gave all of Cappadocia to Ariobarzanes, adding to that Sophene, which he had intended for Tigranes the Young.

Cleopatra had escaped to Pontus, where she lived the rest of her life. As for King Tigranes, he was buried in Tigranocerta – once a fabulous city, it was then abandoned and its precise location lost in the mists of time. Only the king's appearance on coins minted in his honour had survived.

Tigranes' most favourite son, Artavasdes II, succeeded him and continued to strike silver coinage with Greek legends. He was the epitome of the Hellenistic attainment in Armenia. As a patron of the arts, he increased Hellenization of his urban people and the court culture. While Armenia was a bone of contention between Rome and Parthia, Artavasdes maintained the alliance with the former by virtue of his father's treaty with Pompey. But the new king later changed course and deserted the Romans as he had deep-rooted ties with the Parthians. Being himself of Iranian extraction, he had given his sister to the Parthian prince, Pacorus I, in marriage. Mark Antony, who re-invaded Armenia in 34 BC, captured Artavasdes for having switched sides many times and took him and his family to Alexandria as prisoners. A few years later, he was beheaded by the Egyptian Ptolemaic Queen, Cleopatra VII, for refusing to render homage to her by prostration.

# Epilogue

There were many reasons as to why Tigranes' empire was short-lived. For one, it was a hodgepodge of feudal lords/fiefs, nomad warriors from different tribes, and hundreds of thousands of forcibly transferred inhabitants from the neighbouring states – most of these peoples eventually betrayed Tigranes. Secondly, the borders of his enormous territory were sparsely defended, without much political apparatus to be viable in the face of a major attack. Thirdly, the domestic divisions, including the multiple revolts of the king's sons in the second half of his reign, took much of his attention and time, limiting his ability to prepare for the battle with the Romans. Fourthly, a centralization of power, which was the king's intent – unlikely to bring about in antiquity – might have paved the way for a sustainable empire capable of resisting both the power-hungry ambitions of the nobility and the neighbouring powers.

The only negative aspect of Tigranes' new capital city (Tigranocerta) was the vulnerability of its geographical position in the heart of his empire – a flat land that the

Romans had exploited to launch an attack on him. Although the city was built there to profit from the trade routes, it remained far from the northern Armenian uplands, where the steep mountain ranges and valleys could have formed a natural barrier against the enemy. Moreover, Tigranes did not have enough time to mobilize his army. Though somewhat well-trained, the military lacked logistics, cohesion, control, and discipline.

Actually, the emperor was lulled into a false sense of security, and his ill-prepared massive forces proved no match for the organized Roman army. He did not determine a worthy cause that his soldiers would wish to fight for. Tigranes was a bold opportunist and not exactly an astute leader, otherwise he would not have suffered a defeat. He did not know his enemy (the Roman legions) well enough to adopt a counter-military strategy. Besides, his cataphracts down the Batman River were positioned just behind the right flank of his army at the battle of Tigranocerta – this major mistake for placing an important unit there exposed it to a grave danger.

However, his empire, which was created under favourable regional circumstances, when Rome was distracted by civil conflicts at home, already contained within itself the seeds of its own destruction.

Modern scholars have conflicting views on the alliance of Tigranes and Mithridates and its consequences. Some argue that the former made a serious misjudgement when he allied himself with the Pontic king and a strategic mistake by rejecting Roman demands for his ally's surrender. In contrast, others found their alliance necessary to secure each other's flanks from potential invaders, and indicated that Tigranes should not have allowed the annihilation of Pontus that protected his western flank. There are also scholars who believe that Tigranes' great mistake was his neutrality in the later conflicts between Pontus and Rome; otherwise, together with his ally he would have set up a secure military buffer zone against Rome's expansionist policy in the East.

The big question is: for how long would the so-called zone have been maintained? In ancient times, borders were lawless, deserted regions, delineated by landmark barriers, which the Roman Republic and other nations did not hesitate to exploit for their own interests. However, Tigranes had failed to conclude a proper treaty of alliance with Pontus from the outset, as it proved problematic for his prestige and popularity, especially during the second half of his reign. On the other hand, if it had not been for the personal prestige of Lucullus, and his deep-seated desire for dominion and riches, an invasion of Tigranes' empire might have been spared.

The reality on the ground is that the main protagonists – Tigranes, Mithridates, Lucullus and Pompey – pursued their own imperialistic agendas. The Pontic king and the two Roman generals in particular, having very clear objectives and fixed ideas, were in fierce competition with each other in their respective spheres of influence on the Ancient Asia Minor. Eventually, the clash of their different political ideologies, combined with their egomania, led to violent military confrontations with Mithridates, resulting in the final collapse of his kingdom, which paved the way for the Roman invasion of Tigranes' empire and its fall.

After all, no empire had survived throughout history, due to successive tragic turns of events. Even the Roman

Empire fell and, prior to that, Alexander the Great's, and so forth. They all eventually declined and collapsed because of obsession with imperial overexpansion, absence of a capable successor, depletion of resources, invasions of enemy troops resulting from lack of control of territories, cracks in ruling families, domestic rebellions, or treachery of princes to their fathers, as was the case with Tigranes' and Mithridates' sons. With regard to Tigranes the Great, it was mostly his unpreparedness for the battle, the instability of his political position, and his strategic political mistakes that resulted in the fall of his empire.

# Praise

'An instantly engaging narrative that reads like a novel. The book blends historical accounts with creative dialogue based firmly on what is known of the historical characters in order, as the author notes, to "bring the ancient past to life". This goal is admirably achieved.

The work is historically accurate with a firm command of narrative form, progression, tension, and subject matter. Even though I know Tigranes' story well, I found myself reading this book as though it were an adventure novel and wondering how it might end for the hero.

Highly recommended.'

Joshua J. Mark
Author-Editor *Ancient History Encyclopedia*

# Appendices

# Appendix 1. The term 'talent' (ancient money) with Notes

The term 'talent' in the book denotes an important unit of weight and money used in ancient times by the Greeks, Near-Eastern kingdoms, and Romans. Units of weight of precious metals – gold and silver – represented a sum of money. One talent equalled 26 kilograms of silver. Ultimately, the talent became a unit of coinage, divided into 60 minas, corresponding to 600 drachmas. The value of the talent comparing its value to the present-day currencies is very difficult to confirm. Giving readers a brief overview of cost of living, around five drachmas was the normal wage for a week's work, which was a good salary at the time.

### Note 1.
Although the Work is a balanced study of Tigranes II's imperial reign, the information given on his personality by Roman authors is an absurd falsification of the historical truth to serve their own so-called interests. For one thing, the king was neither disloyal to his people, nor an Oriental barbarian, despite his ambitions of conquest. On the contrary, he had contributed a lot to his country's social, economic and cultural development in a period of Hellenism in the Ancient Near East, and shared those Hellenistic ideals with his long-time ally, Mithridates VI.

### Note 2.
It may seem a little strange to readers that Tigranes, during the last years of his reign, looked back on his royal life and had visions of past events (Chapter 24). The reality is that so

many people in the later part of their lives review past roles and experiences, and sometimes have regrets for their mistakes – ancient kings were no exception.

# Appendix 2. List of early kings of Armenia in Chronological Order

Orontes I Sakavakyats (570–560 BC)
Tigranes Orontid (560–535 BC)
Vahagn (530–515 BC)
Hidarnes I (late 6th century BC)
Hidarnes II (early 5th century BC)
Hidarnes III (middle of the 5th century BC)
Ardashir (2nd half of the 5th century BC)

**Attested satraps**

Orontes (401–344 BC)
Darius Codomannus (344–336 BC)

**Yervandian (Yervanduni or Orontid) Dynasty**

Orontes II (336–331 BC)
Mithranes (331–323 BC)
Neoptolemus Orontid (non-dynastic) (323–321 BC)
Mithranes (321–317 BC)
Orontes III (317–260 BC)
Sames (260–243 BC)
Arsames (243–228 BC)
Xerxes (228–212 BC)
Orontes IV (212–200 BC)

## Artashesian (Artaxiad) Dynasty

Artaxias I (190–159 BC)
Artavasdes I (159–120 BC)
Tigranes I (120–95 BC)
Tigranes the Great (Tigranes II, 95–55 BC)
Artavasdes II (55–34 BC)
Artaxias II (33–20 BC)
Tigranes III (20–10 BC)
Tigranes IV with Erato (10 BC–2 BC)

# Appendix 3. Kingdom of Armenia or Major Armenia (map)

# Appendix 4. The banner of Artaxiad dynasty

# Appendix 5. Tigranes' empire (map)

# Appendix 6. The battlefield at Tigranocerta (sketch)

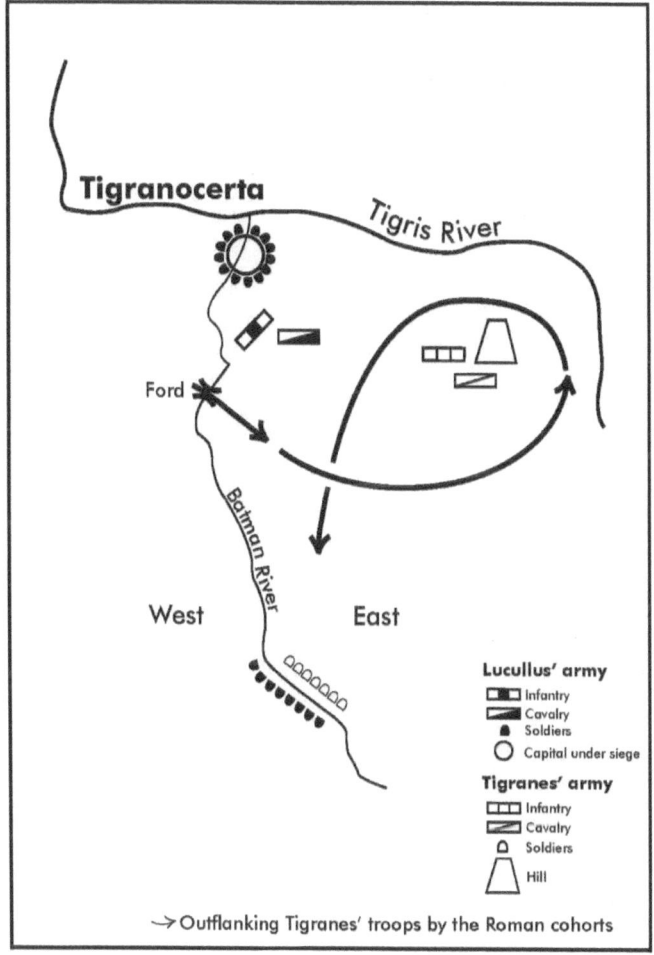

# Appendix 7. Silver coins of King Tigranes II

Tigranes II "the Great" (95-56 B.C.), Kingdom of Armenia, Silver Tetradrachm, Diadem and draped bust of Tigranes II facing right, wearing an Armenian tiara ornamented with a star between two eagles. On the reverse side is Tyche of Antioch seated right on a rock, holding a palm-branch, river god Orontes swimming below to right, monogram on rock and in field

# Appendix 8. Tigranes II with his coin struck in Antioch

# Appendix 9. Bust of Tigranes the Great and his coin

# Appendix 10. Diademed Bust of Tigranes II the Great with his coin of grain ear with leaves

**Appendix 11. Bust of Tigranes the Younger (left). The tyche holding wreath in her right hand (right)**

# Appendix 12. Artavasdes II 56-34 BC

# Appendix 13. Zoroastrian Fire Altars

# Appendix 14. Kingdom of Pontus
(Mithridates VI's Black Sea dominion in 115/114 BC)

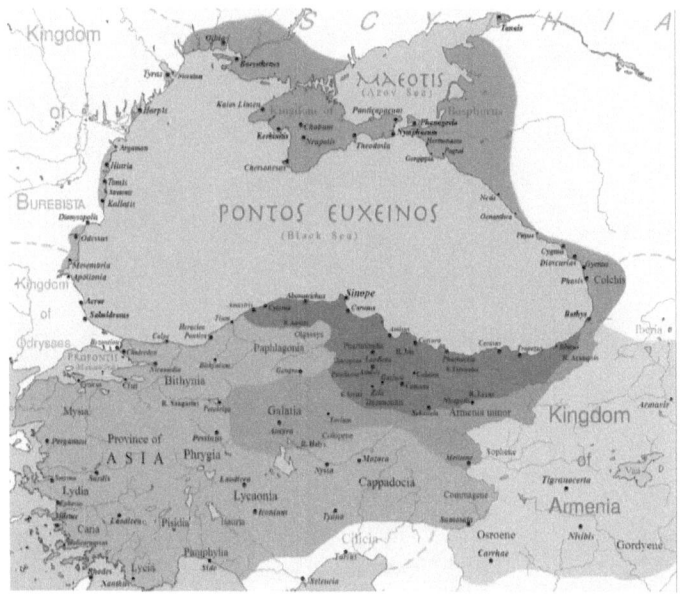

www.ingramcontent.com/pod-product-compliance
Lightning Source LLC
Chambersburg PA
CBHW021149080526
44588CB00008B/276